Have students find the four spelling words hidden in the cover illustration.

SPELLING

Grade 2
Teacher's Edition

Nancy Roser
Professor, Language and Literacy Studies
Department of Curriculum and Instruction
The University of Texas at Austin

SRA

Macmillan/McGraw–Hill

Columbus, Ohio

Printed in the United States of America

SRA
Macmillan/McGraw-Hill
250 Old Wilson Bridge Road, Suite 310
Worthington, Ohio 43085

ISBN 0-02-686188-7

2 3 4 5 6 7 8 9 10 POH 01 00 99 98 97 96 95 94

Contents

Program Components..T4
Program Philosophy T5
Program Features T6
A Teaching Plan T11
Scope and Sequence...T12
Lesson

1	Spelling the Short *a* Sound	...............................T14
2	Spelling the Short *i* Sound	...............................T16
3	Spelling the /o/ and /ô/ Sounds	...........................T18
4	Spelling the Final /k/ Sound	...............................T20
5	Spelling the /nd/ and /st/ Sounds	..........................T22
6	Review	...........................T24
7	Spelling the Short *e* Sound	...............................T26
8	Spelling the Short *u* Sound	...............................T28
9	Spelling Words with *dr*, *tr*, and *gr*	.....................T30
10	Spelling Words with *gl*, *bl*, and *pl*	....................T32
11	Spelling Words That End with *sk*, *mp*, and *ng*	...........T34
12	Review	...........................T36
13	Spelling the Long *a* Sound	................................T38
14	Spelling the Long *e* Sound	................................T40
15	Spelling the Long *i* Sound	................................T42
16	Spelling the Long *o* Sound	................................T44
17	Spelling the /ü/ Sound	.....................................T46
18	Review	...........................T48
19	Spelling Words with *wh* and *sh*	...........................T50
20	Spelling Words with *ch* and *th*	...........................T52
21	Spelling the Vowel + *r* Sound	..............................T54
22	Spelling More Vowel + *r* Sounds	............................T56
23	Easily Misspelled Words	....................................T58
24	Review	...........................T60
25	Spelling Words with *br*, *fr*, and *tr*	.....................T62
26	Spelling Words with *sl* and *sp*	...........................T64
27	Spelling Words Ending with *-s*	.............................T66
28	Spelling Words That Sound Alike	............................T68
29	Spelling Family Names	......................................T70
30	Review	...........................T72
31	Spelling the /u̇/ Sound	.....................................T74
32	Spelling Words Ending in *-ed* and *-ing*	...................T76
33	Spelling the /ou/ Sound	....................................T78
34	Spelling Compound Words	....................................T80
35	Spelling Number Words	......................................T82
36	Review	...........................T84

SRA Spelling Word List Grade 2 ....T86
Using the Mini Lessons with Invented Spelling T88
Answers for Crossword Puzzles and Review Tests T89
Crossword Puzzles T90-T95
Review Tests...T96-T101
Home Study Word Lists...T102-T116
Test-Study-Test Master...T117
Student Progress Chart T118

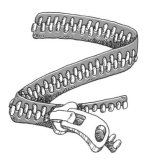

SRA Spelling provides a philosophically sound spelling program with a down-to-earth focus on reading and writing.

Proven Strategies

Motivating Activities

and the Good Sense to Put Spelling in its place.

Professional and Balanced Approach

their   there   they're
- direct, systematic instruction in those high-frequency words that can haunt writers into adulthood

drop the final e before adding -ing
- measured attention to those reliable spelling patterns and rules

Mercury   Venus   Earth
- content-based lessons that provide opportunities to apply word knowledge to interesting words with random spelling patterns

Support for Integrated Learning

WORDS and MEANINGS
- every word in a reading context so spelling has meaning

Prooofreding prakticee
(proofreading practice)
- integrating spelling and proofreading into the writing process

WRITE ON YOUR OWN
- an opportunity to write spelling words in a meaningful context in every lesson

Mini Lessons
- teacher support for instruction as well as flexible tools for capitalizing on "teachable moments"

Word Play

REVIEW

- riddles, brain teasers, and puzzles that conceal serious linguistic discovery, while building a life-long love of words and language

**Student Edition
Grades 1-6**

**Teacher's Guide
Grades 1-6**

**Cover Posters
Grades 1-6**

**Word List Posters
Grades 1-6**

Hang Word List Poster here

**2 Spelling the
Short *i* Sound**

CORE
1. if
2. fix
3. pin
4. his
5. mix
6. rip
7. kiss
8. hid
9. tip
10. milk

CHALLENGE
11. dish
12. mitt
13. fish
14. rich
15. wish

SPELLING

Other Spelling Materials available from SRA

Word Cards
Dolch Popper Words (Grades 1-6)
Dolch Picture Word Cards (Grades 1-6)
Dolch Sight Phrase Cards (Grades 1-6)
Dolch Group Word Teaching Game
(Grades 1-6)

Puzzles
Noun Puzzles (Grades 1-3)
Verb Puzzles (Grades 1-3)
Prefix Puzzles (Grades 3-6)
Suffix Puzzles (Grades 3-6)

Software
Alphabet Circus (Grades K-2)
helps teach letter recognition,
alphabetical order, text creation, and
problem solving. Available in Apple II,
IBM PC/Tandy, and Commodore
64/128 formats.

Spelling Mastery (Grades 1-3)
helps children learn basic spelling and
word recognition skills. Available in
Apple II format.

Spelling Wiz (Grades 1-8)
gives children motivating practice in
spelling more than 300 commonly
misspelled words. Available in Apple II,
IBM PC/Tandy, and Commodore
64/128 formats.

For information call toll free 1-800-843-8855 or write to
SRA
Macmillan/McGraw-Hill
P.O. Box 543
Blacklick, Ohio 43004-0543

SRa SPELLING

Philosophy

SRA Spelling is designed to help your students
- perceive spelling as a meaningful and important part of reading and writing,
- learn to spell those words and patterns essential to literacy,
- develop an ability to examine words critically so students acquire a life-long ability to spell.

To accomplish these goals SRA Spelling
- identified the most frequently used words from student reading and writing found in reliable research,[1]
- organized words and patterns to foster maximum opportunities for students at different developmental stages of spelling to generalize about sounds, letters, and structural patterns,[2]
- included vocabulary of selected content and curricular areas to maintain high interest and allow students to apply their word knowledge to a random group of high-interest words,
- developed a balanced and practical teaching plan to put spelling in meaningful contexts for students and provide focused, manageable support for today's reading and writing instruction,
- designed motivating, fun activities that encourage students to enjoy language while they learn how to spell.

[1] *The Dolch 220 Basic Sight Words;* Hanna, Hanna, Hodges, and Rudorf: *Phoneme-Grapheme Correspondences and Cues to Spelling Improvement;* Harris and Jacobson: *Basic Reading Vocabularies;* Smith and Ingersoll: *Children's Writing Vocabulary.*

[2] Hanna, Hodges, and Hanna: *Spelling : Structure and Strategies;* Henderson and Beers: *Developmental and Cognitive Aspects of Learning to Spell;* Read: *Children's Categorization of Speech Sounds in English;* Read: *Children's Creative Spelling.*

Using SRA Spelling

For Students

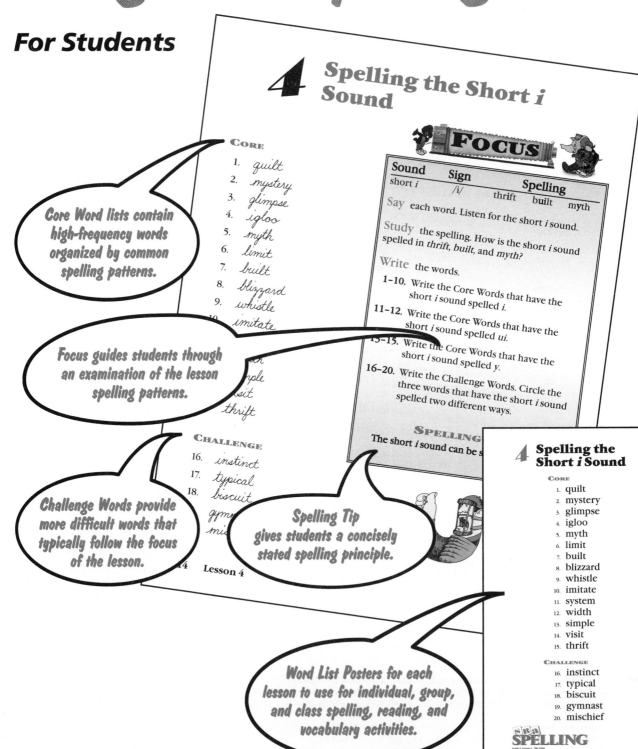

4 Spelling the Short _i_ Sound

CORE

1. quilt
2. mystery
3. glimpse
4. igloo
5. myth
6. limit
7. built
8. blizzard
9. whistle
10. imitate

ple
sit
thrift

CHALLENGE

16. instinct
17. typical
18. biscuit
    gym
    mis

Lesson 4

Core Word lists contain high-frequency words organized by common spelling patterns.

Focus guides students through an examination of the lesson spelling patterns.

Challenge Words provide more difficult words that typically follow the focus of the lesson.

Spelling Tip gives students a concisely stated spelling principle.

Word List Posters for each lesson to use for individual, group, and class spelling, reading, and vocabulary activities.

FOCUS

Sound	Sign	Spelling		
short _i_	/i/	thrift	built	myth

Say each word. Listen for the short _i_ sound.

Study the spelling. How is the short _i_ sound spelled in _thrift_, _built_, and _myth_?

Write the words.

1–10. Write the Core Words that have the short _i_ sound spelled _i_.

11–12. Write the Core Words that have the short _i_ sound spelled _ui_.

13–15. Write the Core Words that have the short _i_ sound spelled _y_.

16–20. Write the Challenge Words. Circle the three words that have the short _i_ sound spelled two different ways.

SPELLING
The short _i_ sound can be s

4 Spelling the Short _i_ Sound

CORE

1. quilt
2. mystery
3. glimpse
4. igloo
5. myth
6. limit
7. built
8. blizzard
9. whistle
10. imitate
11. system
12. width
13. simple
14. visit
15. thrift

CHALLENGE

16. instinct
17. typical
18. biscuit
19. gymnast
20. mischief

SRA SPELLING

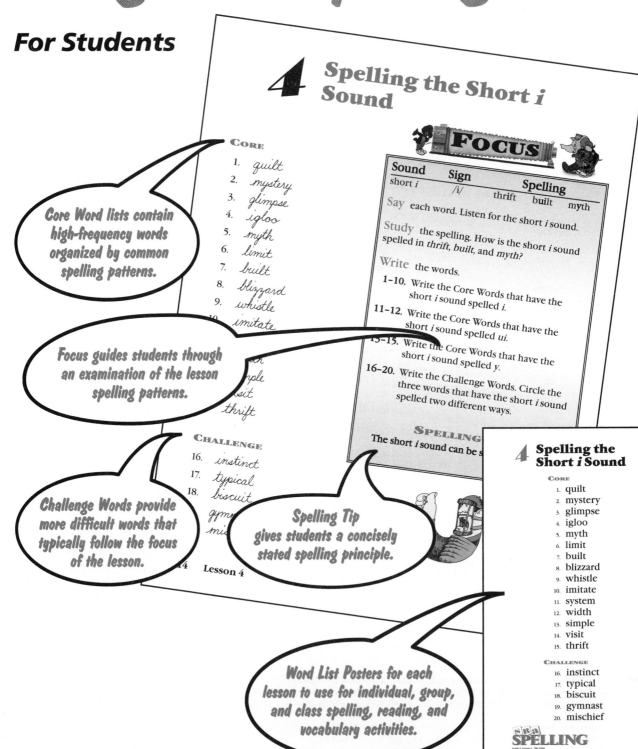

T6

4 Spelling the Short *i* Sound

Objectives
- to learn three spellings of the short *i* sound and apply them to both reading and writing
- to correctly add the adjective suffixes -*ous* and -*y* to nouns
- to learn and practice proofreading skills

Mini Lesson

Objective
- to discover three spellings for the short *i* sound

Write the following sentence on the board.

Who was guilty in that mystery?

Ask students to read the sentence aloud and identify the three words that have the short *i* sound they hear in *simple*. (*guilty, in, mystery*) Have a volunteer come to the board and circle the letter or letters that spell the short *i* sound in each word. (*ui* in *guilty*, *i* in *in*, *y* in *mystery*)

Then ask students to make up sentences containing several words with the short *i* sound. Write *i, ui, y,* and *other* on the board. As students say their sentences, write each word with the short *i* sound under the appropriate heading. If they need help, provide them with one or more of the following words: *grim, filter, build, syrup,* and *gym*.

Review Words

fifth   bridge   quick   citizen   picnic

Write the Review Words on the board. Have students write the Review Word that fits in each group as you read the other words aloud.

1. tunnel, road, railing, _____ (bridge)
2. fast, swift, fleet, _____ (quick)
3. voter, civic, American, _____ (citizen)
4. second, third, fourth, _____ (fifth)
5. blanket, outdoors, eat, _____ (picnic)

Challenge Words

instinct   typical   biscuit   gymnast   mischief*

Have students write the Challenge Word that matches each of these [as you] read aloud.

1. It's a dog's reward. (biscuit)
2. It's what cats use to find th[eir] home. (instinct)
3. It's what gets you into tro[uble]. (mischief)
4. [...]

Mini Lessons help students discover the lesson word pattern or capitalize on teachable moments.

Home Study Words masters for each lesson give students a convenient list for study with family members.

Challenge Words activities can be used with selected students or the entire class.

Review Words in the Teacher's Edition (Grades 3-6) help students recall and spell familiar words with the lesson pattern.

Words from Reading and Writing can be added to the Home Study Words.

SPELLING Home Study Words

4 Spelling the Short *i* Sound

CORE
1. quilt
2. mystery
3. glimpse
4. igloo
5. myth
6. limit
7. built
8. blizzard
9. whistle
10. imitate
11. system
12. width
13. simple
14. visit
15. thrift

CHALLENGE
16. instinct
17. typical
18. biscuit
19. gymnast
20. mischief

WORDS FROM READING AND WRITING

21. _____
22. _____
23. _____
24. _____
25. _____

103

More for Students

Write the Core Words that best complete the story.

An Igloo Is Built

The idea of a house made of snow seems magical, like something out of a fairy tale or (1). But if you ever (2) the arctic region, you may get a (3) of a real snowhouse. It is called an (4).

Igloos are (5) from blocks of snow. Why people built with snow is not a (6). In fact, the reason is (7). There is a (8) to the resources available in arctic areas. Snow is the only resource that does not have to be used with great (9).

To build an igloo, you can (10) the same method or (11) some animals use when they burrow holes in the snow for warmth. You just have to kno___ ___ust what height and (12) to make the ___ ___ snow.

An igloo is the best kind of shelter to be in during an arctic (13). When the winds (14) across the snowy plains, an igloo can keep you as cozy as a soft, warm (15).

Words and Meanings puts Core Words in meaningful story contexts. Students clarify meaning and make important connections between reading, writing, and spelling.

Adjective Suffixes -ous and -y

Change each noun to an adjective by ad___ the suffix -ous or -y. If the noun ends in___ change the final y to i before adding th___ suffix.

16. mystery
17. thrift
18. might

19. glory
20. fruit

**Lesso___

Word Works provides a variety of activities that help students discover spelling patterns in word families.

Decode the Blocks Each snow block holds a word and a number. If the number in a block is 1, write down the first letter of the word in the block. If the number is 2, write down the second letter, and so on. Then unscramble the letters from the row of blocks and write a Core Word.

dove 1	fish 4	mile 2	rows 3	stem 2
curb 2	leap 1	grin 3	bait 4	quit 1
pipe 2	into 1	vote 3	poem 4	else 2
halo 4	urge 3	open 1	slot 2	thin 3
___t 3	chin 3	gift 2	save 3	loot 4

___ns the syllable

___ts each clue.

14. It ha___ ___w.
15. It has an *i*, a *t*, and an *m* but no *l*.

16   Lesson 4

Word Play provides puzzles and brain teasers that conceal important spelling pattern analysis.

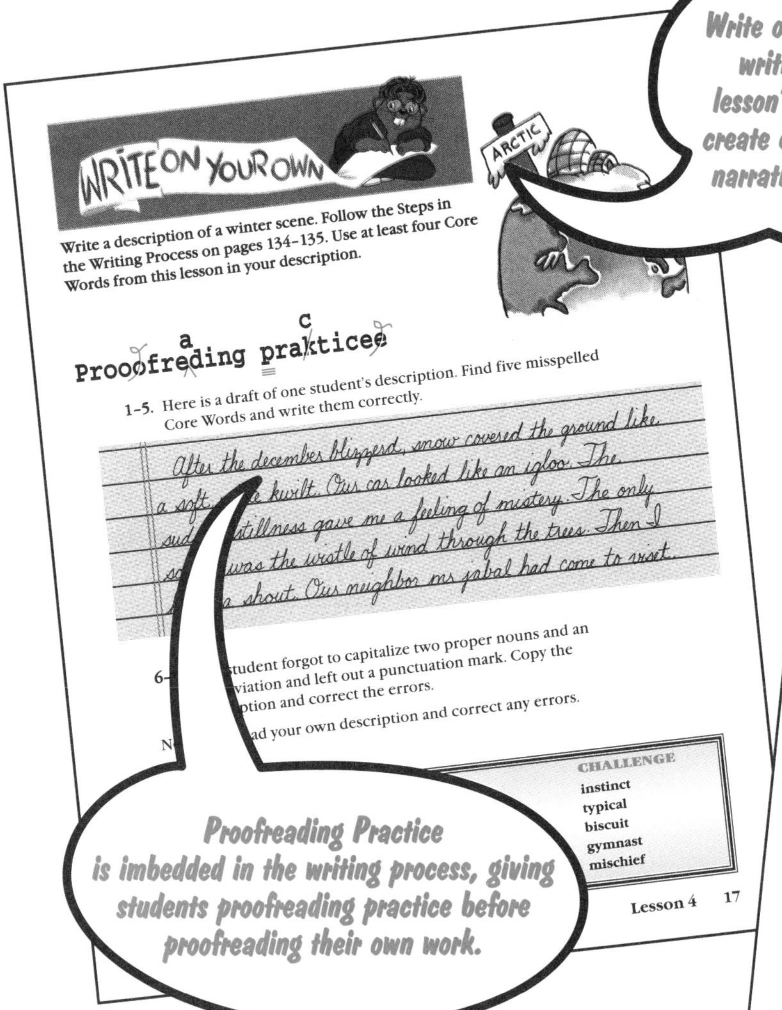

Prooofreding praktices

a — c

(handwritten corrections above: "a" over the crossed-out letter, "c" over the crossed-out letter)

1–5. Here is a draft of one student's description. Find five misspelled Core Words and write them correctly.

> After the decembers blizzerd, snow covered the ground like a soft, white kwilt. Our car looked like an igloo. The sudden stillness gave me a feeling of mistery. The only sound was the wistle of wind through the trees. Then I heard a shout. Our neighbor mrs jabal had come to visit.

6–   A student forgot to capitalize two proper nouns and an abbreviation and left out a punctuation mark. Copy the description and correct the errors.

Now   read your own description and correct any errors.

CHALLENGE
instinct
typical
biscuit
gymnast
mischief

Lesson 4   17

Write on Your Own suggests independent writing opportunities related to the lesson's Words and Meanings. Students create expressive, descriptive, expository, narrative, persuasive, or poetry writing.

Proofreading Practice is imbedded in the writing process, giving students proofreading practice before proofreading their own work.

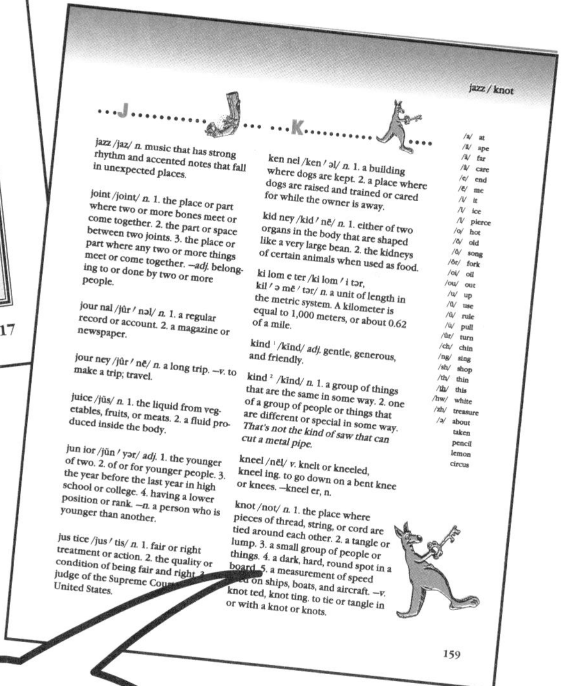

Speller Dictionary includes all Core, Challenge, and Review Words presented at each grade.

Steps in the Writing Process on page T134-T135 help students plan their writing.

Speller Dictionary page

jazz / knot

· · · J · · · · · · · · · ·   · · · K · · · · · · · · · ·

jazz /jaz/ *n.* music that has strong rhythm and accented notes that fall in unexpected places.

joint /joint/ *n.* 1. the place or part where two or more bones meet or come together. 2. the part or space between two joints. 3. the place or part where any two or more things meet or come together. —*adj.* belonging to or done by two or more people.

jour nal /jûr ′ nəl/ *n.* 1. a regular record or account. 2. a magazine or newspaper.

jour ney /jûr ′ nē/ *n.* a long trip. —*v.* to make a trip; travel.

juice /jüs/ *n.* 1. the liquid from vegetables, fruits, or meats. 2. a fluid produced inside the body.

jun ior /jün ′ yər/ *adj.* 1. the younger of two. 2. of or for younger people. 3. the year before the last year in high school or college. 4. having a lower position or rank. —*n.* a person who is younger than another.

jus tice /jus ′ tis/ *n.* 1. fair or right treatment or action. 2. the quality or condition of being fair and right. 3. a judge of the Supreme Court of the United States.

ken nel /ken ′ əl/ *n.* 1. a building where dogs are kept. 2. a place where dogs are raised and trained or cared for while the owner is away.

kid ney /kid ′ nē/ *n.* 1. either of two organs in the body that are shaped like a very large bean. 2. the kidneys of certain animals when used as food.

ki lom e ter /ki lom ′ i tər, kil ′ ə mē ′ tər/ *n.* a unit of length in the metric system. A kilometer is equal to 1,000 meters, or about 0.62 of a mile.

kind ¹ /kind/ *adj.* gentle, generous, and friendly.

kind ² /kind/ *n.* 1. a group of things that are the same in some way. 2. one of a group of people or things that are different or special in some way. *That's not the kind of saw that can cut a metal pipe.*

kneel /nēl/ *v.* knelt or kneeled, kneel ing. to go down on a bent knee or knees. —kneel er, *n.*

knot /not/ *n.* 1. the place where pieces of thread, string, or cord are tied around each other. 2. a tangle or lump. 3. a small group of people or things. 4. a dark, hard, round spot in a board. 5. a measurement of speed used on ships, boats, and aircraft. —*v.* knot ted, knot ting. to tie or tangle in or with a knot or knots.

/ᴀ/	at
/ā/	ape
/ä/	far
/â/	care
/e/	end
/ē/	me
/i/	it
/ī/	ice
/î/	pierce
/o/	hot
/ō/	old
/ô/	song
/ôr/	fork
/oi/	oil
/ou/	out
/u/	up
/ū/	use
/ü/	rule
/u̇/	pull
/ûr/	turn
/ch/	chin
/ng/	sing
/sh/	shop
/th/	thin
/ᵺ/	this
/hw/	white
/zh/	treasure
/ə/	about
	taken
	pencil
	lemon
	circus

159

T9

More for the Teacher

Sentence Dictation Tests can be used for Pretests and Retests. Students can write the entire sentence or just the individual words at the teacher's discretion.

Answers to the Exercises provides answers and assessment tips for all student activities.

Notes give teachers extra information about the spelling patterns of the spelling words.

Sentence Dictation Test

Because the vocabulary in these sentences is within reach of most students at this level, you may have students write the entire sentence. However, if you prefer, you may have students simply write the underlined spelling words.

Core Words

1. Making a <u>quilt</u> is not <u>simple</u>.
2. This <u>myth</u> is about a boy and a bear.
3. How did the <u>mystery</u> end?
4. We must <u>limit</u> the <u>width</u> of the
5. An <u>igloo</u> is <u>built</u> from blocks
6. Our number <u>system</u> is very o
7. I can <u>imitate</u> a train's <u>whistle</u>.
8. Did you <u>glimpse</u> the sun after t
9. Your <u>thrift</u> helps you save for a ra
10. Our cousins are paying us a <u>visit</u>.

Review Words

11. Ken is just entering the <u>fifth</u> grade.
12. Take a <u>quick</u> look at this news story.
13. Every adult <u>citizen</u> has the right to vote.
14. Our <u>picnic</u> spot is just across the <u>bridge</u>.

Challenge Words

15. Birds know how to fly by <u>instinct</u>.
16. A <u>typical</u> puppy gets into some <u>mischief</u>.
17. Try some jam on your <u>biscuit</u>.
    The <u>gymnast</u> did an amazing flip.

Notes

* There are two short *i* sounds in the Challenge Word *mischief*. One is in the first syllable and is spelled *i*. The other is in the second syllable and is spelled *ie*. The second spelling of the short *i* sound is not studied in this lesson.

Lesson 4

Answers to the Exercises

Focus
page 14
1–10. glimpse, igloo, limit, blizzard, whistle, imitate,
5. visit
6. blizzard
7. whistle
8. mystery
9. simple
10. system

4. igloo
5. built
6. mystery
7. simple
8. limit
9. thrift
10. imitate
11. system
12. width
13. blizzard
14. whistle
15. quilt

...ary. ...d use ...Words.

This description offers an opportunity to have students work on writing fresh and interesting similes. When students have completed the assignment, ask them to use their descriptions to write a new ending for the sentence, "Snow covered the ground like a ...."

Word Works
16. mysterious
17. thrifty
18. mighty
19. glorious
20. fruity

Proofreading Practice
1–5. blizzard, quilt, mystery, whistle, visit
6. December
7. Jabal
8–9. Mr.

Word Play
page 16
1. width
2. quilt
3. limit
4. igloo

SRA SPELLING Test-Study-Test

Lesson _____

	Pretest	Self Check and Correct	Retest
1.			
2.			
3.			
4.			
5.			
6.			
7.			
8.			
9.			
10.			
11.			
12.			
13.			
14.			
15.			

T117

Test-Study-Test masters provide a convenient way to pretest and retest students on the lesson words.

SRA SPELLING Review Test Lesson 6

Name _____

Each item below gives three possible spellings of a word. Choose the correct spelling. Mark your answer.

Sample. a. tiger   b. tigur   c. tieger

1. a. gis   b. gas   c. gase
2. a. snak   b. snack   c. snac
3. a. het   b. hayt   c. hat
4. a. map   b. mep   c. mape
5. a. los   b. lost   c. lohst
6. a. milk   b. mylk   c. milke
7. a. kyss   b. kus   c. kiss
8. a. stacke   b. stak   c. stack
9. a. spot   b. spet   c. spaht
10. a. dog   b. dag   c. dawg
11. a. laht   b. lat   c. lot
12. a. laste   b. lat   c. last
13. a. fas   b. fust   c. fast
14. a. sik   b. syck   c. sick
15. a. hes   b. his   c. hys
16. a. mad   b. med   c. nad
17. a. pond   b. pind   c. pond
18. a. typ   b. tep   c. tip
19. a. jub   b. job   c. johb
20. a. lock   b. loack   c. locke

Answers a b c

T96

Review Tests in a standardized-test format can be used as an alternative Pretest or Retest for all Review Lessons.

SRA SPELLING Lesson 6

Name _____

Use Core Words from Lessons 1–5 to complete this puzzle.

ACROSS
3. to flap loosely
4. food between meals
6. tear
7. not thin
8. fuel for car
10. mend or repair
12. thin wood
13. use a bucket and shovel with this

DOWN
1. ___ and on
2. has its own key
4. a stain
5. to go from one side to another
7. mist
9. something you drink
11. touch with lips

T90

Crossword Puzzles for fun and practice for all Review Lessons.

A Teaching Plan

Most teachers prefer to use a weekly five or three session teaching plan for spelling. The chart below can be used to plan the assignments in *SRA Spelling*.

3-Day Plan	5-Day Plan	Activities
1	1	Pretest, Self-Check and Correct Mini Lesson Say, Study, Write Home Study Words Words from Reading and Writing
	2	Words and Meanings Word Works Challenge Words Activity
2	3	Word Play Review Words Activity
	4	Write on Your Own Proofreading Practice
3	5	Retest

Scope and Sequence

Numbers refer to Lessons.

	Grade 1	Grade 2	Grade 3	Grade 4	Grade 5	Grade 6
SPELLING						
Readiness						
Visual Discrimination of Letter Forms	1-3					
Sound to Letter Association, Consonants	4-10					
Sound to Letter Association, Short Vowels	11-16					
Consonant Spellings						
Consonant Blends	22, 24, 31, 36	5-6, 9-12, 25-26, 30	14, 18, 25, 30		13, 18	
Consonant Digraphs	32-33, 36	19-20, 24	27, 30	13, 18		7, 12
Alternate Spellings for /f/, /j/, /k/, and /s/		4, 6	19-20, 24	9-10, 12, 14, 16, 18	32, 36	5, 6, 15, 18
Double Consonants			10, 12, 15, 18	28	34-35	4, 6
Silent Consonants			32-33, 36	29-30	31, 36	
Vowel Spellings						
Short Vowels	17-21, 24	1-3, 6-8, 12	1-2, 6	7, 12	1-6	1, 6
Long Vowels	25-30	13-16, 18	3-4, 6	1-6	7-9, 12	2, 6, 10, 12
Common Spellings for /ô/		3, 6	9, 12		3, 6	3, 6
Common Spellings for /ů/		31, 36				
Common Spellings for /ü/		17-18	5-6	5-6	9, 12	10, 12
Common Spellings for /oi/			7, 12	8, 12		
Common Spellings for /ou/		33, 36	8, 12	8, 12	14, 18	
Common Spellings for Vowel before *r*		21-22, 24	26, 30-31, 36	19, 24, 31, 36	10, 12, 16, 18	8, 12
Common Spellings for /ə/ Unstressed Syllables and Endings			11-12	7, 12, 25, 30	15, 18, 21, 24, 26, 27, 30	9, 12, 14, 18
Spellings Related to Meaning and Word Structure						
Contractions			16, 18, 28, 30			
Compound Words		34, 36	34, 36	34, 36	28, 30	
Homophones		28, 30	22, 24	23-24	17-18	
Adding -***ing***, - ***ed***, and Other Inflectional Endings		32, 36	13, 18, 21, 24	20, 24, 26, 30, 35-36	19, 24	
Plurals and Possessives		27, 30	21, 24	15, 18, 21, 24	20, 22, 24	
Prefixes				22, 24, 33, 36	25, 30	16, 18, 21, 24, 27, 29-30, 32-33, 36
Suffixes				17-18, 27, 30, 32, 36	27, 30, 33, 36	14, 18-20, 24-26, 30-31, 36
Other Spellings						
Mixed or Unique Patterns	23, 24, 34, 36	23-24	17-18	29-30	11-12	13, 18, 28, 30
Content Based Lists	35, 36	29-30, 35-36	23-24, 29, 30, 35-36	11-12, 28, 30	23-24, 29-30, 34-36	11-12, 17-18, 22-24, 34-36

Numbers refer to Lessons.

MEANING AND SPELLING

	Grade 1	Grade 2	Grade 3	Grade 4	Grade 5	Grade 6
Cloze Activities	17-23, 25-29, 31-35	1-5, 7-11, 13-17, 19-23, 25-29, 31-35	1-5, 7-11, 13-17, 19-23, 25-29, 31-35	1-5, 7-11, 13-17, 19-23, 25-29, 31-35	1-5, 7-11, 13-17, 19-23, 25-29, 31-35	1-5, 7-11, 13-17, 19-23, 25-29, 31-35
Homophones and Homographs		13-14, 23, 25, 35	5, 26, 32	3	7	7, 28
Compound Words		16, 19	11, 29	2	8, 28, 35	
Plurals	23, 26, 34	3, 10, 27, 31	19, 21, 33	10, 13, 21		
Parts of Speech and Possessives		5, 17, 22, 26, 29, 33-34	1, 8, 10, 16, 22-23, 25, 27, 34	1, 8-9, 14, 16, 19-20, 26, 31, 35	4, 9, 11, 19, 22, 27	3, 10, 14, 16, 20, 23, 25
Synonyms and Antonyms		2, 4, 8, 15	2, 4, 9, 17		5, 33	4, 26, 31
Base and Inflected Forms of Words		7, 9, 11, 20-21	3, 7, 10, 13	20	1-2, 9-11, 19, 20	3
Syllabication and Hyphenation			15	7, 25, 28, 34		
Word Building with Phonograms	17-22, 24-25, 27-33, 35, 36	32	31			
Prefixes, Suffixes, and Roots			14, 20	4-5, 15, 17, 22, 27, 29, 31-33, 35	3-4, 10, 13-17, 20-21, 23, 25-26, 29, 31-34	1-2, 5, 8-10, 16-17, 19, 20-22, 25, 27, 29, 32-35
Abbreviations and Contractions		28	28, 35	11, 23		

PROOFREADING

	Grade 1	Grade 2	Grade 3	Grade 4	Grade 5	Grade 6
Spelling Errors	17, 23, 26, 30, 32, 34	1-5, 7-11, 13-17, 19-23, 25-29, 31-35	1-5, 7-11, 13-17, 19-23, 25-29, 31-35	1-5, 7-11, 13-17, 19-23, 25-29, 31-35	1-5, 7-11, 13-17, 19-23, 25-29, 31-35	1-5, 7-11, 13-17, 19-23, 25-29, 31-35
Capitalizing First Word in Sentence	19, 29, 36	9, 15, 20, 27	8, 10, 14, 17, 19, 26	8, 15, 25	2, 8, 15, 26, 32	7
Capitalizing Proper Nouns			23, 35	2, 27, 35	4, 9, 13, 15, 20, 26, 35	4, 15, 21
Punctuation	21, 29, 36	3, 5, 10, 13, 17, 23, 25, 29, 34	2-4, 15, 21, 31	1, 5, 7, 10, 20, 31	2, 4, 8-9, 13, 15, 20, 23, 26, 32, 35	4, 7, 21, 27, 35

DICTIONARY

	Grade 1	Grade 2	Grade 3	Grade 4	Grade 5	Grade 6
	18, 20, 22, 25, 27-28, 30, 31, 33, 35, 36	2, 7, 10, 13, 15, 17, 20, 22, 32	3, 5, 10, 13, 20, 22, 27, 29, 32, 34	1, 3, 5, 7, 8, 10, 15, 17, 19, 25, 29, 32-33	1, 3, 5, 8, 10, 13, 15, 17, 20, 23, 25, 27, 29, 32, 34	3, 5, 7, 9, 11, 15, 17, 20-21, 26, 29, 32, 34-35

WRITING OPPORTUNITIES

	Grade 1	Grade 2	Grade 3	Grade 4	Grade 5	Grade 6
Advertisements and Announcements		16		4, 9, 29	9, 20, 26, 33	5, 9
Descriptions	17, 20-22, 26-28, 33-35	29, 34	2	17, 34	4, 10, 14, 33	8, 13, 20-21
Explanations and Directions	29, 31-32	8	14, 17	19, 25	2, 11, 29	22, 32
Interview Questions		17	3, 21	5, 7	32	1
Journals and Diaries		20	1, 32	1, 15, 20	8, 21	3, 10, 27
Letters and Invitations		3, 10, 23, 28	5, 9, 16, 19, 33-34	2, 13, 23, 33, 35	5, 28	2, 7, 25, 31, 35
Lists, Charts, or Posters		2, 4-5, 11, 21-22, 33	11, 15, 23, 29, 35	11, 14, 32	13, 23, 34-35	11, 15, 23, 33
Stories and Personal Narratives	18-19, 23, 25	1, 9, 25, 35	4, 7, 20, 22, 25-26, 31	3, 8, 10, 16, 21, 27,	7, 16, 19, 31	4, 14, 28, 32
Poems and Songs		7, 13-15, 19, 26, 27, 31, 32	8, 13	28	1, 17	17
Reports and Reviews			27	22, 26, 31	3, 22, 25, 33	26, 34
Comparison and Contrast			10			16
Speeches and Dialogue			28		15, 27	19, 29

1 Spelling the Short *a* Sound

Objectives
- to learn a common short *a* spelling and apply it to both reading and writing
- to use word families or phonograms to build new words
- to learn and practice proofreading skills

Mini Lesson

Objective
- to discover a common spelling for the short *a* sound

Draw three boxes (☐☐☐) on the chalkboard. Ask students to listen carefully for the beginning and ending sounds they hear in *bat* as you say the word several times. Have a volunteer write the letters that spell the beginning and ending sounds in the appropriate boxes on the chalkboard. Say *apple* and *bat* several times. Ask students if these two words have the same vowel sound. Tell students this sound is called the short *a* sound. Then ask them how it is spelled. (with an *a*) Have a volunteer add the vowel to the word on the chalkboard.

Then as you say each word below, have students raise their hands if they hear the short *a* sound that they heard in *bat*. Ask a volunteer to write that word on the chalkboard and ring the letter that spells the vowel sound. If students have difficulty spelling the words, allow them to invent the spellings.

> pat man met fat hill gas bad hot lap has map mitt

When all the appropriate words have been written, have students check the spelling of the words with the lesson word list.

Challenge Words

as jam dash
path cash

Have students close their books and write the Challenge Word that matches each of the following clues. When they have finished, have them check their words and spellings.

1. It is something you spread on bread. (*jam*)
2. It starts with *p* and means a *trail*. (*path*)
3. It rhymes with *mash* and means *money*. (*cash*)
4. It rhymes with *has*. (*as*)
5. It rhymes with *lash* and means *to move fast* or *rush*. (*dash*)

Sentence Dictation Test

The vocabulary in these dictation sentences is within reach of most students at this level. You may have students write the entire sentence using invented spellings for words they are uncertain about or have students simply write the underlined spelling words.

Core Words

1. A dog sat in my <u>lap</u>.
2. The <u>map</u> is on the desk.
3. My dad felt <u>bad</u>.
4. May I <u>pat</u> the dog?
5. A big <u>man</u> sat on the bus.
6. The bus needs <u>gas</u> to run.
7. She <u>has</u> a cap.
8. Her cat is <u>fat</u>.
9. They are <u>mad</u> at me.
10. I like the <u>hat</u>.

Challenge Words

11. We made a lot of <u>jam</u>.
12. Stay on the <u>path</u>.
13. She is <u>as</u> tall as I am.
14. He has <u>cash</u> with him.
15. Did you see the cat <u>dash</u> away?

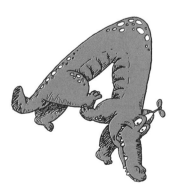

Spelling the Short *i* Sound

Objectives
- to learn a common spelling for the short *i* sound and apply it to both reading and writing
- to recognize the opposites of some words
- to learn and practice dictionary and proofreading skills

Mini Lesson

Objective
- to discover a common spelling for the short *i* sound

Tell students that you are going to say three words, one at a time. Have volunteers give the opposite of each word: **out, small, her** (in, big, him).

Ask students what sound is common in *in, big,* and *him.* Write *in, big,* and *him* on the chalkboard. Ask which word begins with the short *i* sound. Then ask students to tell how the short *i* sound is spelled. (with an *i*) Have volunteers ring the letter that spells the short *i* sound in the other words.

Then have each student write the letter *i* on a piece of paper. Read the pairs of words below, stopping after each pair. Ask students to hold up their papers if they hear the short *i* sound in both words.

his-had   pin-win   of-if   tip-rip   did-hid   fix-fox   miss-kiss   mix-mask

Read the pairs of words again. Have volunteers write the words with the short *i* sound on the chalkboard and ring the letter that spells the vowel sound. If students have difficulty spelling the words, allow them to invent the spelling.

Challenge Words

dish   mitt   fish
rich   wish

Tell students you will be reading pairs of sentences to them. The second sentence in each pair will be missing a word. They are to decide what the missing Challenge Word is and spell it. When you have finished, have them check their words and spellings.

1. A person wears a glove.
    A baseball player wears a _____. (mitt)
2. You put milk in a glass.
    You put food in a _____. (dish)
3. Someone with no money is poor.
    Someone with a lot of money is _____. (rich)
4. There are wings on a bird.
    There are fins on a _____. (fish)
5. You throw a line in the water to catch a fish. You throw a coin in a well to make a _____. (wish)

Sentence Dictation Test

The vocabulary in these dictation sentences is within reach of most students at this level. You may have students write the entire sentence using invented spellings for words they are uncertain about or have students simply write the underlined spelling words.

Core Words

1. I will not go <u>if</u> it rains.
2. Can you <u>fix</u> the bike?
3. Please give me a <u>kiss</u>.
4. How did the page <u>rip</u>?
5. A <u>pin</u> is in the hat.
6. Will you <u>mix</u> the paint?
7. The dog <u>hid</u> the bone.
8. I like <u>milk</u>.
9. This bag is <u>his</u>.
10. I did not <u>tip</u> the cup.

Challenge Words

11. The <u>dish</u> is in the sink.
12. My cat ate a big <u>fish</u>.
13. The king is <u>rich</u>.
14. Did you make a <u>wish</u>?
15. Use a <u>mitt</u> if you play.

Focus
page 6
1–10. (i)f, f(i)x, p(i)n, h(i)s, m(i)x, r(i)p, k(i)ss, h(i)d, t(i)p, m(i)lk
11–15. d(i)sh, m(i)tt, f(i)sh, r(i)ch, w(i)sh

Words and Meanings
page 7
1. his
2. fix
3. rip
4. tip
5. mix
6. milk
7. pin
8. hid
9. kiss
10. if

Word Works
11. his
12. big
13. fix
14. sit
15. in

Word Play
page 8
1–2. fix, mix
3–4. kiss, milk
5. pin
6–7. rip, tip
8. tip
9. his
10. if
11. hid
12. fix
13. mix
14. hid
15. kiss
16. if

Write on Your Own
page 9
Lists will vary. Students should use three Core Words. Use this activity to check for students' ability to use capitalization and punctuation.

Proofreading Practice
1–3. Fix, if, kiss

Spelling the /o/ and /ô/ Sounds

Objectives
- to learn a common spelling for the /o/ and /ô/ sounds and apply them to both reading and writing
- to form plurals of some words
- to learn and practice proofreading skills

Mini Lesson
Objective
- to discover a common spelling for the /o/ and /ô/ sounds

Ask students to think of a word that rhymes with *hot* and is something we use to cook food in. (pot) Repeat the two words *hot* and *pot* several times. Ask students if they hear the same middle sound in both words.

Ask students to think of a word that rhymes with *log* and is often a pet. (dog) Repeat the procedure above. Since there is no name for this sound, it can be referred to as the vowel sound in *dog* or /ô/.

Write the groups of words on the chalkboard, one group at a time. Have students read each group aloud. Ask a volunteer to ring the two words that rhyme in each group.

dog	log	rag	met	got	hot	cross	mess	toss
job	sob	jab	flop	dip	top			

Challenge students to think of other words that rhyme with *dog, hot, toss, job,* or *top*. As students suggest other rhyming words, have volunteers write them in the appropriate group on the chalkboard. Conclude by asking students how the vowel sound is spelled in each word. (with an *o*)

Challenge Words

robin   soggy   slot

cross   cot

Write the following sentences on the chalkboard or dictate them aloud. Have students write the missing Challenge Word in each sentence. When they have finished, have them check their words and spellings.

1. Have you ever slept on a _____ ? (cot)
2. Do you look both ways when you _____ the street? (cross)
3. A _____ flew over my head. (robin)
4. Put a dime in the _____ in the piggy bank. (slot)
5. My towel is very _____. (soggy)

Sentence Dictation Test

The vocabulary in these dictation sentences is within reach of most students at this level. You may have students write the entire sentence using invented spellings for words they are uncertain about or have students simply write the underlined spelling words.

Core Words

1. I <u>got</u> a cap.
2. My <u>dog</u> runs fast.
3. We sat on the <u>log</u>.
4. I like my <u>job</u>.
5. The dog fell <u>off</u> the rock.
6. We need a <u>lot</u> of help.
7. Can you see in the <u>fog</u>?
8. Will you <u>jog</u> later?
9. The cat likes to <u>flop</u> on the bed.
10. A <u>spot</u> is on my hat.

Challenge Words

11. A <u>robin</u> is in the nest.
12. I lay on the <u>cot</u>.
13. The boat can <u>cross</u> the lake.
14. Can the mail fit in the <u>slot</u>?
15. The bag is <u>soggy</u>.

Focus
page 10
1–10. l(o)g, g(o)t, d(o)g, j(o)b, l(o)t, f(o)g, fl(o)p, sp(o)t, j(o)b, (o)ff
11–15. r(o)bin, s(o)ggy, sl(o)t, cr(o)ss, c(o)t

Words and Meanings
page 11
1. job
2. got
3. lot
4. dog
5. fog
6. spot
7. log
8. off
9. jog
10. flop

Word Works
11. logs
12. spots
13. pots
14. hogs
15. frogs
16. tots

Word Play
page 12
1. flop
2. job
3. off
4. spot
5. log
6. lot
7. fog
8. dog
9. jog
10. got

Write on Your Own
page 13
Letters will vary. Students should use three Core Words. Check for students' ability to include parts of a friendly letter.

Proofreading Practice
1–3. job, lot, spot
4–5. . . . job.
. . . dirt.

4 Spelling the Final /k/ Sound

Objectives
- to learn the *ck* spelling for the final /k/ sound and apply it to both reading and writing
- to recognize words with the same or similar meanings
- to learn and practice proofreading skills

Mini Lesson

Objective
- to discover the *ck* spelling for the final /k/ sound

Show a rock, stick, and pen to students. Ask them to name each object. Have a volunteer point to and say the names of the two objects that end with the same last sound. (rock, stick) Have students listen for the last sound in *rock* and *stick* as you point to each object and say the word several times. Then write the sentences on the chalkboard one at a time.

> Tick tock says the clock.
>
> Pack a snack in a sack.
>
> Kick the rock off the dock.
>
> The sock is in back of the rack.

Have students read each sentence aloud, one at a time. Ask volunteers to identify the words in each sentence that have the same last sound as they hear in *rock* and *stick*. Have a volunteer ring the words with the same last sound and say the words aloud. Ask students to study the words that are ringed. Do they all end with the same sound? Do they end with the same two letters? Then pick up the rock and the stick again. Challenge them to spell the words *rock* and *stick*.

Challenge Words

click   flock   shack

clock   backpack

Have students close their books and write the Challenge Word that matches each of these clues. When they have finished, have them check their words and spellings.

1. It is something you use to tell time. (clock)
2. It is something you carry when you go camping. (backpack)
3. It is a group of sheep. (flock)
4. It is a hut. (shack)
5. It is the sound a lock makes when it closes. (click)

Sentence Dictation Test

The vocabulary in these dictation sentences is within reach of most students at this level. You may have students write the entire sentence using invented spellings for words they are uncertain about or have students simply write the underlined spelling words.

Core Words

1. The cage has a <u>lock</u>.
2. I ate a <u>snack</u>.
3. The ship is at the <u>dock</u>.
4. Who hit the gate with a <u>stick</u>?
5. Someone threw a <u>rock</u>.
6. I bought a <u>pack</u> of gum.
7. I tossed the weeds in a <u>sack</u>.
8. My dog is <u>sick</u>.
9. Where is the <u>stack</u> of maps?
10. Can you <u>kick</u> the can?

Challenge Words

11. That <u>clock</u> is made of pine.
12. See the <u>flock</u> of sheep.
13. Lee has a <u>backpack</u>.
14. We rode to the <u>shack</u>.
15. The lock will <u>click</u>.

Focus
page 14
1–10. ro(ck), ki(ck), sa(ck), do(ck), pa(ck), si(ck), sta(ck), lo(ck), sti(ck), sna(ck)
11–15. cli(ck), flo(ck), sha(ck), clo(ck), backpa(ck)

Words and Meanings
page 15
1. dock
2. sick
3. stack
4. kick
5. rock
6. snack
7. pack
8. sack
9. stick
10. lock

Word Works
11. stick
12. sack
13. rock
14. stack
15. sick
16. snack

Word Play
page 16
1. lock
2. sick
3. stick
4. kick
5. stack
6. pack
7–9. stack, stick, snack
10–13. sack, pack, stack, snack
14–16. rock, dock, lock
17–18. stack, stick

Write on Your Own
page 17
Lists will vary. Students should use three Core Words. Check for students' understanding of logical time order.

Proofreading Practice
1–3. Kick, stick, dock

5 Spelling the /nd/ and /st/ Sounds

Objectives
- to learn the spelling for final /nd/ and /st/ sounds and apply them to both reading and writing
- to understand that certain words describe nouns
- to learn and practice proofreading skills

Mini Lesson

Objective
- to discover the spelling for final /nd/ and /st/ sounds

Draw the outline of a hand on the chalkboard. Ask students what you have drawn. Write the word *hand* on the outline, putting one letter in each of the four fingers. Pronounce the word *hand* then ask the class to say it. Erase the first two letters and replace them with *p* and *o* to form the word *pond.* Pronounce the word as before. Repeat the words *hand* and *pond* several times, then ask the students if they hear the same two sounds at the end of each word. Ask if they see the same two letters at the end of the word. Conclude by asking them how they think the last two sounds are spelled.

Repeat the procedure with the words *fist* and *fast,* writing the letters on the knuckles of an outline of a fist.

Have students write *nd* on one piece of paper and *st* on another piece of paper. Ask them to raise the paper with the letters that go with the ending sounds in the word you will read to them. Warn them that some words will not have either sound. Then read the following words aloud.

| sand | lost | card | wind | land | hit | fast | miss | word |

Challenge Words

cast   stand   past
wind   land

Have students close their books and write the Challenge Word that completes each sentence. When they have finished, have them check their words and spellings.

1. When you get up, you _____. (stand)
2. Leaves blow off of trees when there is a lot of _____. (wind)
3. Things that happened long ago are in the _____. (past)
4. Something that you do with a fishing pole is _____. (cast)
5. You plant a garden on your _____. (land)

Sentence Dictation Test

The vocabulary in these dictation sentences is within reach of most students at this level. You may have students write the entire sentence using invented spellings for words they are uncertain about or have students simply write the underlined spelling words.

Core Words

1. Mix the red <u>and</u> blue.
2. Did you hurt your <u>hand</u>?
3. Can you run <u>fast</u>?
4. We like to play in the <u>sand</u>.
5. Who made a <u>list</u>?
6. There are fish in the <u>pond</u>.
7. They play in the <u>band</u>.
8. We <u>just</u> planted the beets.
9. I came in <u>last</u> in the race.
10. I <u>lost</u> my backpack.

Challenge Words

11. She will <u>cast</u> the line into the lake.
12. The jet did not <u>land</u>.
13. We ran <u>past</u> the shack.
14. I had to <u>stand</u> on the bus.
15. The <u>wind</u> just came up.

Answers to the Exercises

Focus
page 18

1–10. sa(nd), po(nd), lo(st), ju(st), a(nd), la(st), li(st), ba(nd), fa(st), ha(nd)

11–15. ca(st), sta(nd), pa(st), wi(nd), la(nd)

Words and Meanings
page 19

1. lost
2. just
3. pond
4. sand
5. hand
6. fast
7. last
8. band
9. and
10. list

Word Works

11. band
12. sand
13. hand
14. pond

Word Play
page 20

1. pond
2. list
3. lost
4. hand
5. fast
6. fast
7. just
8. hand
9. band
10. sand
11. just
12. fast
13. and
14. list
15. last

Write on Your Own
page 21

Posters will vary. Students should use three Core Words. Check that students have used correct spelling in their posters.

Proofreading Practice

1–3. lost, band, pond
4. . . . Toby?

6 Review

- to recall and spell representative Core and Challenge Words from Lessons 1–5
- to demonstrate a knowledge of words and spelling principles in standardized testing formats

Challenge Words Game

Objective
- to review spelling patterns in Lessons 1–5

The following game can be played with the entire class or with selected students. Another strategy is to divide students into two teams and play the game competitively.

The object of the game is to be the first student or team to identify a Challenge Word and spell it correctly from a series of clues that you read one at a time.

If a student or team is the first to call out the word and write it correctly on the chalkboard, that student or team is awarded 2 points.

If another student or team challenges the word or the spelling and corrects the error, that student or team is awarded 5 points. However, if they challenge the word or the spelling, and the word is correct, that student or team loses 2 points.

Here are some possible words and their clues. You may wish to create additional ones. You might also have students make up a set of clues to try on the class.

Challenge Words and Clues

mitt	clock	robin
1. You wear this on your hand.	1. This word has two /k/ sounds.	1. You begin to see this in spring.
2. The last two letters in this word are the same.	2. It has two hands.	2. It is a two-syllable word.
3. This word rhymes with "hit."	3. The first /k/ sound is spelled c.	3. The first syllable has the vowel sound you hear in job.
4. The vowel sound is a short i.	4. The second /k/ sound is spelled ck.	4. It is a type of animal.
5. You use this to play baseball.	5. It tells you the time.	5. It lives in a nest.

Sentence Dictation Test

Each sentence below contains a spelling word studied in this Review Lesson. You may wish to have students write the entire sentence using invented spellings for the other words in the sentence or have students write only the underlined words.

Core Words

1. The car needs some <u>gas</u>.
2. At the zoo we saw a <u>lot</u> of seals.
3. We ate a <u>snack</u> at home.
4. Do not go too <u>fast</u>.
5. We cannot find the <u>map</u>.
6. It must be <u>lost</u>.
7. Is <u>his</u> cap red?
8. The man has a <u>spot</u> on his lip.
9. It looks like <u>milk</u>.
10. I like your <u>hat</u>.
11. My <u>dog</u> wags his tail.
12. Give your mom a <u>kiss</u>.
13. This is my <u>last</u> plum.
14. Put your books on the <u>stack</u>.
15. She is never <u>sick</u>.

Challenge Words

16. Make a <u>wish</u>!
17. She walked down the <u>path</u>.
18. The rain made the grass <u>soggy</u>.
19. A <u>shack</u> was near the road.
20. The team will <u>stand</u> at the bus stop.

Answers to the Exercises

1. gas	9. lot
2. hat	10. sick
3. map	11. snack
4. kiss	12. stack
5. milk	13. lost
6. his	14. last
7. spot	15. fast
8. dog	

Additional Assessment

Standardized-format Test

This Review Lesson may also be evaluated using the black-line master test in a standardized test format on page T96.

Words from Reading and Writing

You may wish to have students exchange their lists of words from reading and writing on the Home Study Words form and test each other.

Crossword Puzzle

For additional practice with the words from the previous five lessons, have students complete the crossword puzzle that appears as a black-line master on page T90.

7 Spelling the Short e Sound

Objectives
- to learn a common spelling for the short e sound and apply it to both reading and writing
- to form the past tense of some verbs
- to learn and practice dictionary and proofreading skills

Mini Lesson

Objective
- to discover a common spelling for the short e sound

Ask students to name what a chicken lays. (egg) Draw the outline of an egg on the chalkboard. Then ask students to listen carefully for the first sound they hear as you pronounce the word *egg* several times. Then ask them if they hear that same sound in any other words. Read the words and have students clap their hands if they think they hear the first sound in *egg*.

fed	hat	off	met	them	fat	tip	test	kick	dock	send

Read the words again, stopping after each word. If the class thinks they hear the *egg* sound in the word, ask a volunteer to write the word in the outline of the egg on the chalkboard. If students have difficulty spelling the words, allow them to invent the spellings. When all the appropriate words have been written, have students check the spelling of the words with the lesson word list.

Conclude by asking students what the vowel sound in *egg* is called (the short e sound) and how the short e sound is spelled in the words in the lesson.

Challenge Words

pen   mess   stem
mend   west

Have students close their books and write the Challenge Word that matches each of these clues. When they have finished, have them check their words and spellings.

1. It is part of a flower. (stem)
2. It is something you can use to write. (pen)
3. It is what you can do to a ripped shirt. (mend)
4. It is a direction on the compass. (west)
5. It is what a disorderly or dirty room looks like. (mess)

Sentence Dictation Test

The vocabulary in these dictation sentences is within reach of most students at this level. You may have students write the entire sentence using invented spellings for words they are uncertain about or have students simply write the underlined spelling words.

Core Words

1. Did you pass the <u>test</u>?
2. We <u>met</u> at my home.
3. Will you <u>send</u> a note?
4. The chicken laid an <u>egg</u>.
5. Please ask <u>them</u> to help.
6. I <u>fed</u> milk to the cat.
7. It is not time to go <u>yet</u>.
8. May we <u>rest</u> on the cot?
9. My class <u>went</u> on a bus ride.
10. Can you <u>bend</u> your leg?

Challenge Words

11. Pick up the <u>mess</u> in the room.
12. Use a black <u>pen</u>.
13. Will you <u>mend</u> my hat?
14. A rose has a <u>stem</u>.
15. The sun is in the <u>west</u>.

Answers to the Exercises

Focus
page 24
1–10. (e)gg, f(e)d, m(e)t, th(e)m, r(e)st, b(e)nd, y(e)t, t(e)st, w(e)nt, s(e)nd
11–15. p(e)n, m(e)ss, st(e)m, m(e)nd, w(e)st

Words and Meanings
page 25
1. egg
2. met
3. rest
4. went
5. fed
6. bend
7. yet
8. test
9. them
10. send

Word Works
11. rested
12. tested
13. spelled
14. rented
15. pecked

Word Play
page 26
1. met
2. (test)
3. (send)
4. them
5. (rest)
6. egg, fed, bend
7. met
8. went, yet

Write on Your Own
page 27
Poems will vary. Students should use three Core Words. Check for students' ability to use rhyming words.

Proofreading Practice
1–3. met, them, rest

8 Spelling the Short *u* Sound

Objectives
- to learn a common spelling for the short *u* sound and apply it to both reading and writing
- to recognize the synonyms of some words
- to learn and practice proofreading skills

Mini Lesson

Objective
- to discover a common spelling for the short *u* sound

Write these words on the chalkboard in a column:

> man   umbrella   dog

Say each word slowly, emphasizing the first sound as you point to the first letter. Tell students to listen closely to the first sound in each word and repeat the process. Then ask students to make a new word using just the first sound they heard in each word. If they need a hint, ask them what they would get if they mixed dirt and water. After students decide on the word *mud,* circle the first letter in each word on the chalkboard as you say the word *mud.* Ask students to spell the word *mud.* Ask if anyone can tell what the middle sound is called. (the short *u* sound) Ask which letter spells the short *u* sound in *mud.* Have students suggest other words with the short *u* sound and list them on the board.

Challenge Words

> dust   hush   lunch
> rush   bunch

Write the following groups of words on the chalkboard. Tell students to think how the words in each group are alike and then write the missing Challenge Word. When they have finished, have them check their words and spellings.

1. breakfast, supper, _____ (lunch)
2. clean, sweep, _____ (dust)
3. group, crowd, _____ (bunch)
4. hurry, run, _____ (rush)
5. quiet! shhhh! _____ (hush)

Sentence Dictation Test

The vocabulary in these dictation sentences is within reach of most students at this level. You may have students write the entire sentence using invented spellings for words they are uncertain about or have students simply write the underlined spelling words.

Core Words

1. Wash the <u>rug</u> in the van.
2. I fell in the <u>mud</u>.
3. You <u>must</u> fill the pail.
4. The lid is <u>stuck</u>.
5. My bike has <u>rust</u> on it.
6. They took <u>us</u> to the park.
7. <u>Shut</u> the tap in the sink.
8. I hope you have good <u>luck</u>.
9. Will you <u>rub</u> my leg?
10. I felt a <u>tug</u> on the line.

Challenge Words

11. We packed the <u>lunch</u>.
12. Please <u>dust</u> the shelf.
13. You do not need to <u>rush</u>.
14. The <u>bunch</u> of roses is pretty.
15. Who can make the dog <u>hush</u>?

Answers to the Exercises

Focus
page 28
1–10. (u)s, m(u)d, r(u)b, t(u)g, l(u)ck, m(u)st, r(u)g, sh(u)t, r(u)st, st(u)ck
11–15. d(u)st, h(u)sh, l(u)nch, r(u)sh, b(u)nch

Words and Meanings
page 29
1. must
2. mud
3. shut
4. rust
5. rub
6. rug
7. stuck
8. tug
9. luck
10. us

Word Works
11. mud
12. tug
13. shut
14. us
15. rug
16. rub

Word Play
page 30
1. (tug)boat
2. (rub)ber
3. b(us)
4. (shut)ting
5. (luck)y
6. stuck
7. rust
8. mud
9. rug
10. must
11–12. luck, stuck
13–14. tug, rug
15–16. must, rust

Write on Your Own
page 31
Directions will vary. Students should use three Core Words. Check for clarity of directions.

Proofreading Practice
1–3. Shut, rub, rug

9 Spelling Words with *dr, tr,* and *gr*

Objectives
- to learn the spelling for the /dr/, /tr/, and /gr/ consonant blends and apply them to both reading and writing
- to differentiate base words and endings
- to learn and practice proofreading skills

Mini Lesson

Objective
- to discover the spelling for the /dr/, /tr/, and /gr/ consonant blends

Have students guess two words from two hints you will give them. Hint number one is the two words are the sounds you might hear when it rains or when a faucet is leaking. Hint number two is the two words rhyme with *flip* and *flop.* (drip, drop) Then ask students to listen carefully for the first two sounds they hear in *drip* and *drop.* Have a volunteer write the two letters that spell the beginning sounds on the chalkboard. (dr) Repeat the process for *gr* and *tr* using these words: *green grass* and *tree trunk.*

Then write the word parts below on the chalkboard. Have volunteers take turns making words by adding one or more of the blends *dr, tr,* or *gr* to the word parts. Ask them to write each word under the appropriate word part on the chalkboard and then say the word. For example, under *—ade,* students might write *trade* and *grade.*

-ade	-ip	-ain	-ay	-im	-ill	-and	-ab

Challenge Words

dress   trim   grass

try   grow

Have students close their books and write the Challenge Word that rhymes with each clue word. When they have finished, have them check their words and spellings.

1. him (trim)
2. slow (grow)
3. mess (dress)
4. pass (grass)
5. by (try)

Sentence Dictation Test

The vocabulary in these dictation sentences is within reach of most students at this level. You may have students write the entire sentence using invented spellings for words they are uncertain about or have students simply write the underlined spelling words.

Core Words

1. Who <u>drove</u> you home?
2. The cat went up the <u>tree</u>.
3. The <u>truck</u> is green.
4. Can you hit the <u>drum</u>?
5. We went on a <u>trip</u>.
6. She likes to <u>drive</u>.
7. I had a <u>grand</u> time.
8. The baby had a big <u>grin</u> on his face.
9. What <u>grade</u> is she in?
10. Did the rain <u>drip</u> on the mat?

Challenge Words

11. Will you <u>try</u> to fix my bike?
12. Please <u>trim</u> the bush.
13. Will you cut the <u>grass</u>?
14. My <u>dress</u> is new.
15. I like to <u>grow</u> roses.

Focus
page 32
1–10. dr: drip, drum, drive, drove
tr: tree, trip, truck
gr: grin, grade, grand
11–15. (dr)ess, (tr)im, (gr)ass, (tr)y, (gr)ow

Words and Meanings
page 33
1. grade
2. truck
3. tree
4. drip
5. grand
6. drive
7. trip
8. drove
9. drum
10. grin

Word Works
11. drip
12. tree
13. grin
14. truck
15. drum
16. grade

Word Play
page 34
1. drove
2. grand
3. trip
4. grin
5. drip
6. drum
7. grin
8. tree
9. drive
10. grade
11. Drive
12. Truck
13. Grand

Write on Your Own
page 35
Stories will vary. Students should use three Core Words. Check to see if students' stories include a beginning, middle, and ending.

Proofreading Practice
1–3. trip, grand, drove
4–5. We had....
It was.....

10 Spelling Words with *gl, bl,* and *pl*

Objectives
- to learn the spellings for the /gl/, /bl/, and /pl/ consonant blends and apply them to both reading and writing
- to form the plurals of words ending with *-s*
- to learn and practice dictionary and proofreading skills

Mini Lesson

Objective
- to discover the spellings for the /gl/, /bl/, and /pl/ consonant blends

Ask students to listen for the beginning sounds that they hear as you say the word *glad* several times. Then have students look around the classroom to find objects that have the same beginning sounds as *glad*. Ask volunteers to point to the things and say words such as *globe, glass,* and *glue.* If necessary, give students clues to help them find some objects. Write the words on the chalkboard. Ask students what two letters they see at the beginning of each word. (gl) Conclude by asking how the first two sounds of each word are spelled.

Follow the same procedure to introduce the beginning sounds in *blast* and *plum.* Say the words *blast* and *plum* several times. Then ask students to listen for the beginning sounds. Have students look around the classroom to find objects that have the same beginning sounds as *blast* and *plum.* Ask students to point to the things and say the words. If necessary, give students clues to help them find some objects. Write the words on the chalkboard and ask how the beginning sounds are spelled. Example words:

| blue | blocks | black | blotter | plan | plaid | plate | plant |

When all the appropriate words have been written, have volunteers come to the chalkboard to ring the beginning sounds in each word.

Challenge Words

glue   blank   planet
gloves   blanket

Have students close their books and write the Challenge Word that matches each of these clues. When they have finished, have them check their words and spellings.

1. It keeps you warm in bed. (blanket)
2. It is something sticky. (glue)
3. It moves around the sun. (planet)
4. You wear them on your hands. (gloves)
5. It is a space that is not filled in. (blank)

Sentence Dictation Test

The vocabulary in these dictation sentences is within reach of most students at this level. You may have students write the entire sentence using invented spellings for words they are uncertain about or have students simply write the underlined spelling words.

Core Words

1. A <u>plum</u> is purple.
2. Did the rocket <u>blast</u> off?
3. That <u>plot</u> of land is big.
4. Will you <u>blend</u> the paint?
5. Please pass the <u>glass</u>.
6. A <u>block</u> is on top.
7. I am <u>glad</u> you came.
8. We will <u>plan</u> a trip.
9. Can a cat <u>blink</u>?
10. What is five <u>plus</u> ten?

Challenge Words

11. Where are my <u>gloves</u>?
12. Fix the rip with <u>glue</u>.
13. Is that <u>planet</u> red?
14. Fill in the <u>blank</u>.
15. I will nap on the <u>blanket</u>.

Answers to the Exercises

Focus
page 36
1–10. *gl:* glad, glass
bl: blast, blend, blink, block
pl: plan, plus, plum, plot
11–15. (gl)ue, (bl)ank, (pl)anet, (gl)oves, (bl)anket

Words and Meanings
page 37
1. plan
2. glad
3. block
4. plum
5. glass
6. blend
7. plot
8. blast
9. blink
10. plus

Word Works
11. dresses
12. bosses
13. pluses
14. classes
15. messes
16. gases

Word Play
page 38
1–4. plan, plus, plum, plot
5–8. blast, blend, blink, block
9–10. glad, glass
11. plot
12. the main story in a book, play, or movie
13. The outlaws formed a plot to rob the stagecoach.
14. the second meaning
15. plum and plus

Write on Your Own
page 39
Invitations will vary. Students should use three Core Words. Check to see that students have included what, where, when *information in their invitations.*

Proofreading Practice
1–3. plan, glad, plus
4–5. . . . glad.
. . . games.

11 Spelling Words That End with *sk*, *mp*, and *ng*

Objectives
- to learn the spellings for the final /sk/, /mp/, and /ng/ sounds and apply them to both reading and writing
- to add *-ing* to verbs
- to learn and practice proofreading skills

Mini Lesson

Objective
- to discover the spelling for the final /sk/, /mp/, and /ng/ sounds

Ask students what you wear on your face on Halloween. (mask) Have a volunteer name the word. Ask a volunteer to name the letters that spell the ending sounds and to write the word on the chalkboard. Then have a volunteer ring the letters that spell the ending sound. (*sk*)

Repeat the procedure for *lamp* and *spring* with these clues: It is on a table and you turn it on when you want to read. (lamp) It is the season that follows winter. (spring)

Then read the words below, one at a time.

camp	wing	long	desk	song	dump	ask	lamp

Have volunteers write the words with the /sk/, /mp/, and /ng/ sounds under *mask*, *lamp*, or *spring* on the chalkboard. (*sk: desk, ask; mp: camp, dump, lamp; ng: wing, long, song*) When all the appropriate words have been written, have students check the spelling of the words with the word list.

Challenge Words

blimp   task   stamp
bring   grump

Write the following sentences on the chalkboard. Have students write the missing Challenge Word in each sentence. When they have finished, have them check their words and spellings.

1. Did you put a _____ on the envelope? (stamp)
2. A large _____ flew in the sky. (blimp)
3. Please _____ me the mail. (bring)
4. Washing the car is an easy _____. (task)
5. Do not be a _____ at the party. (grump)

Sentence Dictation Test

The vocabulary in these dictation sentences is within reach of most students at this level. You may have students write the entire sentence using invented spellings for words they are uncertain about or have students simply write the underlined spelling words.

Core Words

1. Who has a <u>mask</u>?
2. A bee can <u>sting</u>.
3. <u>Dump</u> the rocks on the sand.
4. I will <u>ask</u> where to go.
5. Can you <u>jump</u> on the log?
6. We went on a <u>long</u> trip.
7. Sit at the front <u>desk</u>.
8. Day <u>camp</u> is fun.
9. Will you sing a <u>song</u>?
10. The bird flapped its <u>wing</u>.

Challenge Words

11. I need a <u>stamp</u>.
12. We rode in the <u>blimp</u>.
13. What is the <u>task</u>?
14. The <u>grump</u> sat in the back.
15. Please <u>bring</u> me a book.

Answers to the Exercises

Focus
page 40
1–3. mask, ask, desk
4–6. camp, dump, jump
7–10. long, sting, wing, song
11–15. bli(mp), ta(sk), sta(mp), bri(ng), gru(mp)

Words and Meanings
page 41
1. camp
2. desk
3. ask
4. sting
5. long
6. wing
7. mask
8. jump
9. song
10. dump

Word Works
11. camping
12. dumping
13. stinging
14. jumping
15. asking

Word Play
page 42
1. camp
2. dump
3. long
4. mask
5. jump
6. wing
7. jump
8. song
9. sting
10. desk
11. ask
12. tell
13. tell
14. ask

Write on Your Own
page 43
Rules will vary. Students should use three Core Words. Check for realistic and logical thinking reflected in the lists of rules.

Proofreading Practice
1–4. jump, dump, long, sting

12 Review

Objectives
- to recall and spell representative Core and Challenge Words from Lessons 7–11
- to demonstrate a knowledge of words and spelling principles in standardized testing formats

Challenge Words Game

Objective
- to review spelling patterns in Lessons 7–11

The following game can be played with the entire class or with selected students. Another strategy is to divide students into two teams and play the game competitively.

The object of the game is to be the first student or team to identify a Challenge Word and spell it correctly from a series of clues that you read one at a time.

If a student or team is the first to call out the word and write it correctly on the chalkboard, that student or team is awarded 2 points.

If another student or team challenges the word or the spelling and corrects the error, that student or team is awarded 5 points. However, if they challenge the word or the spelling, and the word is correct, that student or team loses 2 points.

Here are some possible words and their clues. You may wish to create additional ones. You might also have students make up a set of clues to try on the class.

Challenge Words and Clues

blanket	grass	stamp
1. It keeps you warm.	1. It grows outside.	1. It begins and ends with two consonants.
2. This word has two syllables.	2. The last two letters are the same.	2. It has a short *a* sound in the middle.
3. This word begins like *blast* and rhymes with *bucket*.	3. It has the vowel sound you hear in *fast*.	3. Every letter must have one.
4. The two vowel letters are *a* and *e*.	4. It is usually green.	4. It takes a licking very well.
5. It covers you in bed.	5. This plant covers the ground.	5. It rhymes with *camp*.

Sentence Dictation Test

Each sentence below contains a spelling word studied in this Review Lesson. You may wish to have students write the entire sentence using invented spellings for the other words in the sentence or have students write only the underlined words.

Core Words

1. The hen kept her <u>egg</u> warm.
2. He had <u>mud</u> on his boots.
3. Put the <u>rug</u> down.
4. We looked for a spot to <u>camp</u>.
5. My mom will play the <u>drum</u>.
6. How much is five <u>plus</u> six?
7. All of them passed the <u>test</u>.
8. We must <u>blend</u> blue and yellow to make green.
9. Our cat was <u>stuck</u> in a tree.
10. My dad was <u>glad</u> to help.
11. That is my favorite <u>song</u>.
12. The bird has a nest in this <u>tree</u>.
13. I can see its <u>wing</u> from here.
14. My mother drives a <u>truck</u>.
15. No one is here <u>yet</u>.

Challenge Words

16. Have you seen the <u>glue</u>?
17. I am never late for <u>lunch</u>.
18. We will not make a <u>mess</u>.
19. Please <u>bring</u> more books.
20. I like the blue <u>dress</u>.

Additional Assessment

Standardized-format Test

This Review Lesson may also be evaluated using the black-line master test in a standardized test format on page T97.

Words from Reading and Writing

You may wish to have students exchange their lists of words from reading and writing on the Home Study Words form and test each other.

Crossword Puzzle

For additional practice with the words from the previous five lessons, have students complete the crossword puzzle that appears as a black-line master on page T91.

Spelling the Long *a* Sound

Objectives
- to learn three spellings for the long *a* sound and apply them to both reading and writing
- to identify and write homophones
- to learn and practice dictionary and proofreading skills

Mini Lesson

Objective
- to discover three spellings for the long *a* sound

Draw a simple outline of a pail on the chalkboard. Ask students to name the object. Ask them to listen carefully to the vowel sound they hear in the middle of the word as you repeat the word *pail* several times. Say each pair of words below, one at a time. Ask students to listen for the vowel sound and to decide which of the items has long *a*. Then write the appropriate word in the pail.

grape-pen	letter-hay	map-nail	fan-plate	bed-bait

Ask students to make a list of things with the same vowel sound they hear in *pail*. Then have students read each word aloud. Have the class decide if the word has long *a*. Have the students write the word in the pail. If students have difficulty spelling words with the long *a* sound, allow them to invent the spellings.

Select any three words in the pail that represent the *ai*, *ay*, and *a-e* spellings for the long *a* sound. Pronounce each word and ask students to identify the letters that spell the long *a* sound in each word. Circle the letters after each answer.

Challenge Words

trail   blaze   pain

tray   stain

Have students close their books and write the Challenge Word that matches each of these clues. When they have finished, have them check their words and spellings.

1. *You hike on it.* (trail)
2. *It is dirt.* (stain)
3. *It hurts.* (pain)
4. *It is something to carry food on.* (tray)
5. *It is a fire.* (blaze)

Sentence Dictation Test

The vocabulary in these dictation sentences is within reach of most students at this level. You may have students write the entire sentence using invented spellings for words they are uncertain about or have students simply write the underlined spelling words.

Core Words

1. The <u>plate</u> is filled.
2. Will you <u>raise</u> the flag?
3. A big fish ate the <u>bait</u>.
4. Can you peel a <u>grape</u>?
5. I need a <u>cane</u>.
6. Is the <u>hay</u> in the shed?
7. Who likes to <u>rake</u>?
8. Milk is in the <u>pail</u>.
9. The cat <u>came</u> home.
10. What did you <u>say</u>?

Challenge Words

11. Stay on the <u>trail</u>.
12. Where is your <u>pain</u>?
13. I can see the <u>blaze</u>.
14. There is a <u>stain</u> on the rug.
15. The glass is on the <u>tray</u>.

Focus
page 46
1–10. r(a)k(e), b(ai)t, s(ay), c(a)n(e), p(ai)l, h(ay), pl(a)t(e), r(ai)se, c(a)m(e), gr(a)p(e)
11–15. tr(ai)l, bl(a)z(e), p(ai)n, tr(ay), st(ai)n

Words and Meanings
page 47
1. cane
2. rake
3. hay
4. bait
5. pail
6. say
7. raise
8. came
9. plate
10. grape

Word Works
11. pail, pale
12. tail, tale
13. hey, hay
14. hole, whole
15. plain, plane

Word Play
page 48
1–6. rake, bait, pail, hay, plate, grape
7. grape
8. rake
9. bait or plate
10. say or hay
11. came
12. plate or bait
13. pail
14. cane
15. pail, plate, pole
16. came, clay, crane
17. raise, reel, rust
18. cane, coat, crab

Write on Your Own
page 49
Newspaper stories will vary. Students should use three Core Words. Check that students have written their stories in a logical order of events.

Proofreading Practice
1–4. bait, plate, came, say
5–6. . . . dock.
. . . bait.

14 Spelling the Long *e* Sound

Objectives
- to learn two spellings for the long *e* sound and apply them to both reading and writing
- to identify homographs
- to learn and practice proofreading skills

Mini Lesson

Objective
- to discover two spellings for the long *e* sound

Draw an outline of a long eel on the chalkboard. Ask students to listen carefully for the first sound they hear as you identify the picture and pronounce the word *eel* several times. Write the sentences below on the chalkboard, one at a time. Ask a volunteer to read each sentence and to underline the words that have the same vowel sound they heard in *eel*. Then have the student write the words with long *e* in the outline of the eel. (feet, tree; green, leaf, seat; knee, teeth)

> My feet are next to the tree.
>
> There is a green leaf on my seat.
>
> My knee and teeth hurt.

When all of the words have been written, challenge students to write in more words with the long *e* sound. If students have difficulty spelling the words, allow them to invent the spellings.

Conclude by asking students what the vowel sound in *eel* is called. (the long *e* sound) Then ask how many spellings of the long *e* they see. (two)

Challenge Words

mean   cream   sneeze

leave   sleep

Write the following groups of words on the chalkboard. Tell students to think how the words in each group are alike, and then write the missing Challenge Word. When they have finished, have them check their words and spellings.

1. doze, nap, _____ (sleep)
2. butter, milk, _____ (cream)
3. go, exit, _____ (leave)
4. bad, nasty, _____ (mean)
5. cough, sniffle, _____ (sneeze)

Sentence Dictation Test

The vocabulary in these dictation sentences is within reach of most students at this level. You may have students write the entire sentence using invented spellings for words they are uncertain about or have students simply write the underlined spelling words.

Core Words

1. A <u>wheel</u> fell off the van.
2. Did you fish in the <u>deep</u> sea?
3. Who is on your <u>team</u>?
4. I gave <u>each</u> dog a bone.
5. Will you feed the <u>sheep</u>?
6. They made a nice <u>meal</u>.
7. We have not <u>seen</u> them.
8. I just had a <u>dream</u>.
9. Can you <u>read</u> the name?
10. When will we get a <u>treat</u>?

Challenge Words

11. I must <u>leave</u> at six.
12. The <u>cream</u> is in the bag.
13. Who will <u>sleep</u> on the cot?
14. Dust makes me <u>sneeze</u>.
15. What do you <u>mean</u>?

15 Spelling the Long *i* Sound

Objectives
- to learn three spellings for the long *i* sound and apply them to both reading and writing
- to recognize the antonyms of some words
- to learn and practice dictionary and proofreading skills

Mini Lesson

Objective
- to discover three spellings for the long *i* sound

Ask students to tell what an airplane and bird can both do. (fly) Ask them to tell where they fly. (in the sky) Have students listen carefully for the vowel sound they hear as you repeat *fly* and *sky* several times. Ask them to answer each question with a word that has the same vowel sound as they hear in *fly* and *sky*. As students give answers, write their responses in three columns on the chalkboard according to the spelling of the long *i* sound.

> What is the opposite of day? (night)
> What is the opposite of laugh? (cry)
> What is the opposite of narrow? (wide)

Challenge students to think of other words that have the same vowel sound and write them in the correct columns. Then give students these additional clues and have a volunteer write each answer in the proper column. Ask how many spellings of the long *i* sound they see. (three)

> What is the opposite of left? (right)
> What is the opposite of wet? (dry)
> What is a type of evergreen tree? (pine)

Challenge Words

sly   might   stripe
shy   tight

Have students close their books and write the Challenge Word that is missing in each sentence.

1. My family _____ move to Texas. (might)
2. These shoes are too _____. (tight)
3. I painted a _____ on the kite. (stripe)
4. In most fables, the fox is very clever and _____. (sly)
5. The child in the story is _____. (shy)

Sentence Dictation Test

The vocabulary in these dictation sentences is within reach of most students at this level. You may have students write the entire sentence using invented spellings for words they are uncertain about or have students simply write the underlined spelling words.

Core Words

1. I will shine a <u>light</u>.
2. It rained last <u>night</u>.
3. Will you <u>dry</u> my face?
4. The cat and dog had a <u>fight</u>.
5. We planted a <u>pine</u> tree.
6. My bike is a <u>sight</u>.
7. We will <u>fly</u> a kite.
8. Raise your <u>right</u> hand.
9. Drive in the <u>wide</u> lane.
10. Did you <u>cry</u>?

Challenge Words

11. That fox is <u>sly</u>.
12. There is a <u>stripe</u> on the wheel.
13. The band on my hat is <u>tight</u>.
14. We <u>might</u> run home.
15. The puppy is <u>shy</u>.

Focus
page 54
1–10. p(i)n(e), n(igh)t, cr(y), f(igh)t, w(i)d(e), fl(y), l(igh)t, s(igh)t, dr(y), r(igh)t
11–15. sl(y), m(igh)t, str(i)p(e), sh(y), t(igh)t

Words and Meanings
page 55
1. light
2. fly
3. wide
4. pine
5. night
6. fight
7. cry
8. dry
9. right
10. sight

Word Works
11. night
12. right
13. dry
14. wide
15. cry
16. light

Word Play
page 56
1–2. fly, night
3–4. wide, right
5–6. light, sight
7–8. pine, dry
9. fight
10–12. cry, fly, dry
13–14. pine, wide
15. fly
16. light
17. right
18. pine

Write on Your Own
page 57
Weather reports will vary. Students should use three Core Words. Check for elements of a weather forecast: temperature, sky conditions, and so on.

Proofreading Practice
1–4. dry, night, right, fly
5–7. Today, Clouds, Pilots

16 Spelling the Long *o* Sound

Objectives
- to learn three spellings for the long *o* sound and apply them to both reading and writing
- to write two words to make a compound word
- to learn and practice proofreading skills

Mini Lesson

Objective
- to discover three spellings for the long *o* sound

Ask students to listen carefully to the sentence that you will read. Point out that each sentence has a missing word that rhymes with another word in the sentence. Explain to students that you will say the word *blank* in the place of the missing word. Then ask a volunteer to say aloud the missing word. Write the complete sentence on the chalkboard. Have a volunteer read the sentence aloud and ring the rhyming words.

> *I left the note in my other _____ . (coat)*
>
> *I smelled the rose with my _____ . (nose)*
>
> *The plants will grow in a nice straight _____ . (row)*

Point to the six words that were ringed. Ask students if all six words have the same vowel sound. Ask if anyone can tell what that sound is called. Ask what three ways is that sound spelled in the words and which spelling is used when the long *o* sound comes at the end of a word.

Challenge Words

slow   coach   float
globe   toast

Have students write the Challenge Word that matches each of these clues. When they have finished, have them check their words and spellings.

1. It is what a boat can do. (float)
2. It is not fast. (slow)
3. It is something you eat for breakfast. (toast)
4. It is a round model of the earth. (globe)
5. It is a person who trains sports teams. (coach)

Sentence Dictation Test

The vocabulary in these dictation sentences is within reach of most students at this level. You may have students write the entire sentence using invented spellings for words they are uncertain about or have students simply write the underlined spelling words.

Core Words

1. More <u>snow</u> fell at night.
2. A <u>goat</u> eats grass.
3. Did you wash with <u>soap</u>?
4. The dog has a black <u>nose</u>.
5. A <u>toad</u> sat on a rock.
6. We will <u>row</u> to the dock.
7. Did <u>those</u> cats have a fight?
8. Where is my <u>coat</u>?
9. Please <u>blow</u> the horn now.
10. Can we sail the <u>boat</u>?

Challenge Words

11. Hand me the <u>globe</u>.
12. I like jam on my <u>toast</u>.
13. We rode on the <u>coach</u>.
14. Can you <u>float</u>?
15. A snail is <u>slow</u>.

Answers to the Exercises

Focus
page 58
1–10. c(oa)t, bl(ow), n(o)s(e), b(oa)t, r(ow), th(o)s(e), g(oa)t, s(oa)p, sn(ow), t(oa)d
11–15. sl(ow), c(oa)ch, fl(oa)t, gl(o)b(e), t(oa)st

Words and Meanings
page 59
1. goat
2. toad
3. boat
4. those
5. soap
6. snow
7. blow
8. coat
9. nose
10. row

Word Works
11. sailboat
12. nosedive
13. raincoat
14. snowball
15. toadstool
16. soapsuds

Word Play
page 60
1–2. toad, coat
3–4. boat, row
5–6. soap, goat
7–9. blow, row, snow
10–11. nose, those
12. row

Write on Your Own
page 61
Ads will vary. Students should use three Core Words. Check that students' ads are clearly stated.

Proofreading Practice
1–4. row, goat, snow, blow

17 Spelling the /ü/ Sound

Objectives
- to learn two spellings for the /ü/ sound and apply them to both reading and writing
- to identify words that name places
- to learn and practice dictionary and proofreading skills

Mini Lesson

Objective
- to discover two spellings for the /ü/ sound

Draw the outline of a large rocket ship on the chalkboard. Tell students that you are planning a trip to the moon. Have them listen carefully to the vowel sound they hear in *moon* as you repeat the word several times. Explain to students that you can only bring things with you that have the same vowel sound they hear in *moon*. Tell students that you are going to read two words at a time. Have students decide which word in each pair has the same vowel sound as *moon*. Ask a volunteer to say the word aloud as you write it in the outline of the rocket ship. (tune, pool, boot, broom, tube)

> tune or toy   pole or pool   boot or boat   broom or rug   tube or tire

Challenge students to suggest other words that have the same vowel sound as *moon* and to write them in the outline of the rocket ship.

Conclude by explaining to students that the sign for the vowel sound they hear in *moon* and *tune* is /ü/. Ask students how many spellings of the vowel sound they see in the rocket ship. (two) Have a volunteer circle the letters that spell the /ü/ sound.

Challenge Words

moose   cute*   balloon
shoot   goose

Tell students you will be reading pairs of sentences to them. The second sentence in each pair will be missing a word. They are to decide what the missing Challenge Word is and to spell it. When they have finished, have them check their words and spellings.

1. A pitcher can throw a strike.
   A basketball player can _____ a basket. (shoot)
2. A monster is ugly.
   A baby is _____. (cute)
3. A goat has horns.
   A _____ has antlers. (moose)
4. A duck can quack.
   A _____ can honk. (goose)
5. A boat can float.
   A hot-air _____ can fly. (balloon)

Sentence Dictation Test

The vocabulary in these dictation sentences is within reach of most students at this level. You may have students write the entire sentence using invented spellings for words they are uncertain about or have students simply write the underlined spelling words.

Core Words

1. Did you go to the <u>zoo</u>?
2. I lost my <u>boot</u>.
3. We played a <u>tune</u>.
4. Hand me the <u>tube</u> of paint.
5. It may snow <u>soon</u>.
6. I gave <u>food</u> to the fish.
7. Do you swim in the <u>pool</u>?
8. My dog sleeps in my <u>room</u>.
9. The <u>moon</u> shines at night.
10. I am not <u>rude</u>.

Challenge Words

11. A <u>goose</u> laid an egg.
12. Can you <u>shoot</u> the ball?
13. The <u>balloon</u> landed in the sea.
14. A <u>moose</u> is as big as a truck.
15. There is a <u>cute</u> rag doll.

Answers to the Exercises

Focus
page 62
1–10. t(u)b(e), z(oo),
b(oo)t, f(oo)d,
t(u)n(e), p(oo)l,
s(oo)n, r(u)d(e),
m(oo)n, r(oo)m
11–15. m(oo)se,
c(u)t(e), ball(oo)n,
sh(oo)t, g(oo)se

Words and Meanings
page 63
1. zoo
2. pool
3. room
4. tube
5. tune
6. food
7. rude
8. moon
9. soon
10. boot

Word Works
11. pool
12. zoo
13. room
14. house
15. park
16. lake

Word Play
page 64
1. zoo
2. boot
3. moon
4. pool
5. tune
6. food
7. Pool
8. Moon
9. Food
10. Zoo
11. rail, room, rude
12. soon, stem, sun
13. mean, moon, mule
14. take, trip, tube
15. zebra, zero, zoo

Write on Your Own
page 65
Questions will vary. Students should use three Core Words. Check for correct end punctuation.

Proofreading Practice
1–3. zoo, food, pool
4–5. . . . lions?
. . . pool?

Notes

* The word *cute* has the /ū/ sound rather than /ü/ studied in this lesson. There is a slight difference in the pronunciation of these sounds.

18 Review

Objectives
- to recall and spell representative Core and Challenge Words from Lessons 13–17
- to demonstrate a knowledge of words and spelling principles in standardized testing formats

Challenge Words Game

Objective
- to review spelling patterns in Lessons 13–17

The following game can be played with the entire class or with selected students. Another strategy is to divide students into two teams and play the game competitively.

The object of the game is to be the first student or team to identify a Challenge Word and spell it correctly from a series of clues that you read one at a time.

If a student or team is the first to call out the word and write it correctly on the chalkboard, that student or team is awarded 2 points.

If another student or team challenges the word or the spelling and corrects the error, that student or team is awarded 5 points. However, if they challenge the word or the spelling, and the word is correct, that student or team loses 2 points.

Here are some possible words and their clues. You may wish to create additional ones. You might also have students make up a set of clues to try on the class.

Challenge Words and Clues

stain	globe	sneeze

stain
1. This word begins with two consonants.
2. Ink will do this to a white shirt.
3. The long *a* sound is spelled *ai*.
4. It rhymes with *rain*.
5. This is a dirt spot that won't come clean.

globe
1. It is round.
2. The long *o* sound is spelled *o-e*.
3. It's a kind of map.
4. This word begins with the same two letters as *glow*.
5. This is a round map of the world.

sneeze
1. It's something people usually cannot hold back.
2. It is done through the mouth and nose.
3. It begins with two consonants.
4. It rhymes with *breeze*.
5. The long *e* sound is spelled *ee*.

Sentence Dictation Test

Each sentence below contains a spelling word studied in this Review Lesson. You may wish to have students write the entire sentence using invented spellings for the other words in the sentence or have students write only the underlined words.

Core Words

1. The wind will <u>blow</u> hard today.
2. A full <u>moon</u> is in the sky.
3. They played a <u>tune</u> I love.
4. That store sells <u>bait</u>.
5. The workers washed the <u>plate</u>.
6. We drank milk with our <u>meal</u>.
7. Put on <u>dry</u> socks.
8. I saw her last <u>night</u>.
9. He did not have much to <u>say</u>.
10. The cat dug a <u>deep</u> hole in the sand.
11. The pizza was a great <u>treat</u>.
12. Turn <u>right</u> at the corner.
13. Always wash with <u>soap</u>.
14. We patted the dog on the <u>nose</u>.
15. We met at the <u>zoo</u>.

Challenge Words

16. The firefighter put out the <u>blaze</u>.
17. Add <u>cream</u> to the sauce.
18. The puppy was very <u>shy</u>.
19. Your father is a <u>coach</u>.
20. They bought a <u>balloon</u> at the fair.

Additional Assessment

Standardized-format Test

This Review Lesson may also be evaluated using the black-line master test in a standardized test format on page T98.

Words from Reading and Writing

You may wish to have students exchange their lists of words from reading and writing on the Home Study Words form and test each other.

Crossword Puzzle

For additional practice with the words from the previous five lessons, have students complete the crossword puzzle that appears as a black-line master on page T92.

Spelling Words with *wh* and *sh*

Objectives
- to learn the spellings for the /hw/ or /w/ and the /sh/ sounds and apply them to both reading and writing
- to form compound words
- to learn and practice proofreading skills

Mini Lesson

Objective
- to discover the spellings for the /hw/ or /w/ and the /sh/ sounds

Ask students how they might tell someone to be quiet without saying a word. Hold your finger to your lips to suggest the "shhhh" sound. After students respond with the "shhhh" sound, write the words *shine* and *flash* on the chalkboard and have the class say the words several times. Ask the students if they hear the "shhhh" sound in both words and whether the sound comes at the beginning or end of each word. Ask which letters occur in both words. Then ask a volunteer to circle the letters that spell the /sh/ sound in each word.

Write the three question words *what, why,* and *where* on the chalkboard. Say the words slowly emphasizing the initial sound. Then have the class say the words. Ask if they hear the same beginning sound in each word. Ask if they see the same letters. Ask a volunteer to circle the letters that spell the /hw/ or /w/ sound.

Challenge Words

whisper   shall   share

whiskers   shadow

Have students close their books and write the missing Challenge Word in each sentence.

1. My cat is as quiet as a _____. (whisper)
2. It likes to _____ my dinner. (share)
3. I _____ feed the cat some of my fish. (shall)
4. It will eat in the _____ of the table. (shadow)
5. Then the cat will wash its _____. (whiskers)

Sentence Dictation Test

The vocabulary in these dictation sentences is within reach of most students at this level. You may have students write the entire sentence using invented spellings for words they are uncertain about or have students simply write the underlined spelling words.

Core Words

1. The sun will <u>shine</u>.
2. A <u>flash</u> of light lit up the sky.
3. It is a <u>shame</u> we lost.
4. You can see <u>where</u> the dog hid the bone.
5. We dug clams at the <u>shore</u>.
6. I will wait <u>while</u> you shop.
7. Please tell me <u>why</u> you have to leave.
8. Can you get a <u>shock</u> from the lamp?
9. The <u>clash</u> of the pots made me jump.
10. Did you see <u>what</u> I made?

Challenge Words

11. The tree casts a big <u>shadow</u>.
12. Please <u>whisper</u> while I read.
13. A cat has long <u>whiskers</u>.
14. Will you <u>share</u> your food?
15. What <u>shall</u> I paint?

Focus
page 68
1–4. what, why, where, while
5–10. clash, shame, shine, flash, shock, shore
11–15. (wh)isper, (sh)all, (sh)are, (wh)iskers, (sh)adow

Words and Meanings
page 69
1. why
2. clash
3. where
4. shore
5. shine
6. what
7. flash
8. shock
9. while
10. shame

Word Works
11. flashlight
12. somewhere, somewhat
13. sunshine
14. whatever, wherever
15. shoreline
16. meanwhile

Word Play
page 70
1. while
2. shine
3. shore
4. shock
5–8. shame, shine, shock, shore
9–10. clash, flash
11–14. what, why, where, while
15–17. Sentences will vary. Students should use *what, where,* or *why* in their sentences.

Write on Your Own
page 71
Song lyrics will vary. Students should use three Core Words in their lyrics. Check for rhythm and rhyme in students' song lyrics.

Proofreading Practice
1–3. why, where, shame

Spelling Words with *ch* and *th*

Objectives
- to learn the spellings for the /ch/ and /th/ sounds and apply them to both reading and writing
- to add the suffix *-er* to some words
- to learn and practice dictionary and proofreading skills

Mini Lesson

Objective
- to discover the spellings for the /ch/ and /th/ sounds

Point to your chin and cheek and ask students to name each body part. Ask students if they hear the same beginning sound in both words. Write *chin* and *cheek* on the chalkboard. Then ask students to tell the letters they think spell the /ch/ sound. Have a volunteer circle the answer on the chalkboard.

Then point to your mouth and teeth and ask students to name each body part. Repeat the same procedure with the words *mouth* and *teeth* having students name the letters that spell the sound heard at the end of both words and write them on the chalkboard.

Challenge students to think of other parts of the body that have the /ch/ or /th/ sounds and speculate about the spelling. Possible answers: *chest, thumb, arch.*

Challenge Words

child   thick   reach
chore   think

Have students close their books and write the Challenge Words that go with the clues.

1. Two words that have the same beginning sound as *thank*. (thick, think)
2. Two words that have the same beginning sound as *choke*. (child, chore)
3. One word that has the same ending sound as *teach*. (reach)

Sentence Dictation Test

The vocabulary in these dictation sentences is within reach of most students at this level. You may have students write the entire sentence using invented spellings for words they are uncertain about or have students simply write the underlined spelling words.

Core Words

1. A <u>thin</u> sheet of ice was on the road.
2. I gave my dog a <u>bath</u>.
3. Can you play <u>with</u> me?
4. Gas fumes can make you <u>choke</u>.
5. Please <u>teach</u> me to ice skate.
6. I lost my <u>tooth</u>.
7. You must <u>thank</u> him for his help.
8. What is that <u>thing</u> on the log?
9. We had <u>such</u> a fun time at the zoo.
10. Do not eat too <u>much</u>.

Challenge Words

11. Can you <u>think</u> of her name?
12. It is a <u>chore</u> to wash the dishes.
13. Each <u>child</u> jumped into the pool.
14. The bus crashed in the <u>thick</u> fog.
15. Did the boat <u>reach</u> the shore?

Answers to the Exercises

Focus
page 72
1–4. much, such, choke, teach
5–10. thing, tooth, thank, bath, thin, with
11–15. (ch)ild, (th)ick, rea(ch), (ch)ore, (th)ink

Words and Meanings
page 73
1. with
2. thing
3. much
4. teach
5. bath
6. thank
7. thin
8. tooth
9. such
10. choke

Word Works
11. teacher
12. painter
13. climber
14. catcher
15. speaker

Word Play
page 74
1. much
2. such
3. thin
4. thank
5. teach
6. bath
7. choke
8. tooth
9. bath
10. with
11–15. Answers will vary. Students should use *teach, thank, choke, bath,* and *thing* in their sentences.

Write on Your Own
page 75
Entries will vary. Students should use three Core Words. Check for a beginning, middle, and ending in each diary entry.

Proofreading Practice
1–4. tooth, bath, with, thing
5–6. Today... Suddenly...

21 Spelling the Vowel + *r* Sound

Objectives
- to learn the *ar* spelling for the /är/ sound and apply it to both reading and writing
- to add the suffixes **-er** and **-est** to some words
- to learn and practice proofreading skills

Mini Lesson

Objective
- to discover the *ar* spelling for the /är/ sound

Ask students to tell a word that means the same as automobile (car). Have students listen carefully as you repeat the word *car* several times. Then ask students to tell a word that names something in the sky at night that rhymes with *car*. (star) Have students listen carefully as you repeat *star* several times. Ask students if they hear the same sound in *car* and *star*. (yes) Write *car* and *star* on the chalkboard. Pronounce each word slowly while pointing to the appropriate letters. Ask which letters spell the vowel and *r* sound.

Then read the incomplete phrases, one at a time. Point out that each missing word is the opposite of the first word. Ask a volunteer to write the word on the chalkboard.

stop and _____ (start)	dull and _____ (sharp)
easy and _____ (hard)	whole and _____ (part)
near and _____ (far)	light and _____ (dark)

Challenge Words

arm   march   alarm
smart   harm

Have students close their books and write the Challenge Word that matches each clue.

1. It rhymes with *farm* and means *to scare*. (alarm)
2. It rhymes with *dart* and means *clever*. (smart)
3. It rhymes with *farm* and means *part of your body*. (arm)
4. It rhymes with *farm* and means *to hurt*. (harm)
5. It rhymes with *starch* and means *to walk and step in time*. (march)

Sentence Dictation Test

The vocabulary in these dictation sentences is within reach of most students at this level. You may have students write the entire sentence using invented spellings for words they are uncertain about or have students simply write the underlined spelling words.

Core Words

1. I play in the <u>yard</u>.
2. We live on the <u>farm</u>.
3. Please use the <u>cart</u>.
4. Did you paint in <u>art</u> class?
5. When did the play <u>start</u>?
6. The sky is <u>dark</u>.
7. The team plays in the <u>park</u>.
8. The <u>barn</u> is red.
9. A jay has a <u>sharp</u> bill.
10. The nut is <u>hard</u>.

Challenge Words

11. The band will <u>march</u>.
12. My <u>arm</u> is in a sling.
13. The <u>alarm</u> rang.
14. Is a seal <u>smart</u>?
15. My dog will not <u>harm</u> the cat.

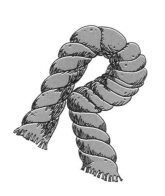

22 Spelling More Vowel + *r* Sounds

Objectives
- to learn the *ir* spelling for the /ûr/ sound and the *or* spelling for the /ôr/ sound and apply them to both reading and writing
- to learn number words
- to learn and practice dictionary and proofreading skills

Mini Lesson

Objective
- to discover the *ir* spelling for the /ûr/ sound and the *or* spelling for the /ôr/ sound

Ask students to name the opposite of *last*. (first) Have students listen carefully as you repeat *first* several times. Repeat the procedure for the opposite of *tall*. (short) Read the words below. Have students raise their hands if they think they hear one of the vowel plus *r* sounds in the word. (The underlined words have the vowel plus *r* sound.)

> dog   <u>short</u>   play   here   <u>first</u>   <u>dirt</u>   seem   <u>short</u>   <u>horse</u>

Write *first* and *short* on the chalkboard. Read the underlined words again. Ask a volunteer to attempt to spell each word with the vowel plus *r* sound. Write the word under *first* or *short* depending on the spelling.

Challenge Words

store   third   morning
dinosaur*   whirl

Have students close their books and write the Challenge Word that matches each of these clues.

1. It is an animal that lived long ago. (dinosaur)
2. It is a place to buy things. (store)
3. It comes after *second*. (third)
4. It is what a top can do. (whirl)
5. It is the beginning of the day. (morning)

Sentence Dictation Test

The vocabulary in these dictation sentences is within reach of most students at this level. You may have students write the entire sentence using invented spellings for words they are uncertain about or have students simply write the underlined spelling words.

Core Words

1. A <u>bird</u> is in the tree.
2. I pushed the <u>dirt</u> back.
3. A <u>horse</u> eats hay.
4. My <u>shirt</u> has red spots.
5. Who came in <u>first</u>?
6. That <u>girl</u> is in my class.
7. The rose is <u>for</u> my pal.
8. I have a <u>horn</u> on my bike.
9. Who picked <u>more</u> grapes?
10. We waited a <u>short</u> time.

Challenge Words

11. My pal is in the <u>third</u> grade.
12. I rode in the truck this <u>morning</u>.
13. Please go to the <u>store</u>.
14. Did you see the <u>dinosaur</u>?
15. The dancer started to <u>whirl</u>.

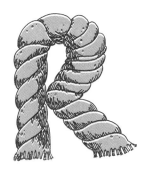

Answers to the Exercises

Focus
page 80
1–5. girl, bird, dirt, first, shirt
6–10. more, horse, horn, short, for
11–15. st(or)e, th(ir)d, m(or)ning, dinos(aur), wh(ir)l

Words and Meanings
page 81
1. horn
2. girl
3. shirt
4. first
5. bird
6. for
7. short
8. horse
9. dirt
10. more

Word Works
11. first
12. second
13. third
14. fourth
15. fifth

Word Play
page 82
1. horse
2. horn
3. bird
4. shirt
5. dirt
6. girl
7. For
8. First
9. More
10. Short
11–12. Answers will vary. Sentences should include *horn* meaning 1. the hard object on the head of some animals, and 2. something used to make a loud sound.

Write on Your Own
page 83
Plans will vary. Students should use three Core Words in their plans. Check that students have written their plans in a logical order.

Proofreading Practice
1–5. for, shirt, horse, bird, more

Notes

* In dinosaur *the vowel plus r sound is spelled aur. The spelling is not studied in this lesson.*

23 Easily Misspelled Words

Objectives
- to learn the spellings of some easily misspelled words and apply them to both reading and writing
- to learn homographs
- to learn and practice proofreading skills

Mini Lesson

Objective
- to discover the spellings of some easily misspelled words

Write the following words on the chalkboard:

fuzz	buzz	does

Ask students to say the words aloud. Ask if the words end with the same sounds. Follow by asking which word is not spelled like the others. (does) Have a volunteer circle the letters in *does* that have a different spelling for the /u/ sound.
Write the following words on the chalkboard:

fur	turn	were

Ask students if they hear the same vowel plus *r* sound in all three words. (yes) Follow by asking which word is not spelled like the others. (were) Have a volunteer circle the letters in *were* that have a different spelling for the /ûr/ sound.

Challenge Words

many   away   goes
kind   both

The following activity can be done as an oral class activity or a silent paper and pencil activity. Tell students you will be reading sentences to them that tell a story. Each sentence will be missing a word, but you will give them a clue to the missing word. They are to decide what the missing Challenge Word is and spell it.

1. Every week my pal _____ bird-watching with me. The missing word rhymes with *froze*. (goes)
2. We _____ love birds. The missing word starts like *boy*. (both)
3. We always see _____ birds on our walk. The missing word rhymes with *penny*. (many)
4. We move quietly so we will not scare them _____. The missing word ends like *day*. (away)
5. Sometimes I can tell the _____ of bird from its call. The missing word rhymes with *find*. (kind)

Sentence Dictation Test

The vocabulary in these dictation sentences is within reach of most students at this level. You may have students write the entire sentence using invented spellings for words they are uncertain about or have students simply write the underlined spelling words.

Core Words

1. The peaches <u>were</u> ripe.
2. We picked <u>every</u> plum.
3. The stove is <u>very</u> hot.
4. Where has the cat <u>gone</u>?
5. We <u>live</u> at the shore.
6. Can you see <u>who</u> is in the store?
7. What is <u>your</u> plan?
8. I can <u>give</u> you a pail.
9. My dog <u>does</u> not need a bath.
10. Do you have <u>any</u> cash?

Challenge Words

11. The bird went <u>away</u>.
12. My pal and I <u>both</u> like to camp.
13. The farmer raises <u>many</u> pigs.
14. Who <u>goes</u> swimming every day?
15. What <u>kind</u> of bird is that?

Focus
page 84
1–10. does, gone, who, any, your, give, very, were, live, every
11–15. many, away, goes, kind, both

Words and Meanings
page 85
1. who
2. your
3. does
4. live
5. every
6. any
7. gone
8. very
9. give
10. were

Word Works
11. Close, close
12. live, live
13. Does, does
14. Wind, wind

Word Play
page 86
1. gone
2. any
3. were
4. give
5. does
6. every
7. live
8. your
9. who
10. very
11. who
12. every
13–15. any, very, every
16. give
17. every
18. very
19. any
20. gone

Write on Your Own
page 87
Postcards will vary. Students should use three Core Words on their postcards. Check for students' ability to use different types of sentences and end punctuation.

Proofreading Practice
1–4. very, give, any, Who
5–6. ...medal? ...races?

Review

Objectives
- to recall and spell representative Core and Challenge Words from Lessons 19–23
- to demonstrate a knowledge of words and spelling principles in standardized testing formats

Challenge Words Game

Objective
- to review spelling patterns in Lessons 19–23

The following game can be played with the entire class or with selected students. Another strategy is to divide students into two teams and play the game competitively.

The object of the game is to be the first student or team to identify a Challenge Word and spell it correctly from a series of clues that you read one at a time.

If a student or team is the first to call out the word and write it correctly on the chalkboard, that student or team is awarded 2 points.

If another student or team challenges the word or the spelling and corrects the error, that student or team is awarded 5 points. However, if they challenge the word or the spelling, and the word is correct, that student or team loses 2 points.

Here are some possible words and their clues. You may wish to create additional ones. You might also have students make up a set of clues to try on the class.

Challenge Words and Clues

shadow

1. It has two syllables.
2. It begins with the same consonant sound as *shine*.
3. This can follow you when you take a walk on a sunny day.
4. It has the short *a* and long *o* vowel sounds.
5. This is the dark shape made by something that blocks the light.

dinosaur

1. It has three syllables.
2. It begins with the same letter as *dog*.
3. The last syllable rhymes with *roar*.
4. This lived on the earth long ago.
5. This is a large, extinct reptile.

whiskers

1. Cats have these.
2. It begins with the same sounds and letters as *whisper*.
3. They grow on people.
4. There is a short *i* sound spelled *i* in the first syllable.
5. Some men shave them off.

Sentence Dictation Test

Each sentence below contains a spelling word studied in this Review Lesson. You may wish to have students write the entire sentence using invented spellings for the other words in the sentence or have students write only the underlined words.

Core Words

1. Do you know <u>where</u> the cat went?
2. The waves splashed on the <u>shore</u>.
3. The crust was very <u>thin</u>.
4. A <u>dark</u> cloud passed over the town.
5. The band played in the city <u>park</u>.
6. He teaches the <u>first</u> grade.
7. We go to the lake <u>every</u> year.
8. You must be <u>very</u> careful crossing the street.
9. A <u>flash</u> of light was seen in the sky.
10. My cat hates her <u>bath</u>.
11. I will <u>teach</u> my sister the game.
12. Be careful with that <u>sharp</u> knife.
13. The <u>girl</u> in the red shoes won the race.
14. Today we saw a <u>short</u> film.
15. Be sure to bring <u>your</u> pen.

Challenge Words

16. We must <u>share</u> the books.
17. This <u>child</u> is next in line.
18. Our family will <u>march</u> in the parade.
19. I will call you in the <u>morning</u>.
20. We saw <u>many</u> fish in the pond.

Additional Assessment

Standardized-format Test
This Review Lesson may also be evaluated using the black-line master test in a standardized test format on page T99.

Words from Reading and Writing
You may wish to have students exchange their lists of words from reading and writing on the Home Study Words form and test each other.

Crossword Puzzle
For additional practice with the words from the previous five lessons, have students complete the crossword puzzle that appears as a black-line master on page T93.

Spelling Words with *br*, *fr*, and *tr*

Objectives
- to learn the spellings for the /br/, /fr/, and /tr/ consonant blends and apply them to both reading and writing
- to understand the multiple meanings of some words
- to learn and practice proofreading skills

Mini Lesson

Objective
- to discover the spellings for the /br/, /fr/, and /tr/ consonant blends

Draw a picture of a tree with apples on the chalkboard. Ask a volunteer to point to the trunk of the tree. Have students listen carefully to the beginning sounds they hear as you say the word *tree* several times. Then ask if they hear the same beginning sounds in *trunk*. Label the drawing by writing *tree* and *trunk*. Have a volunteer circle the two letters that spell the beginning sounds in *tree* and *trunk*. (tr)

Next point to a branch on the tree and ask students to identify it. Have students listen carefully to the beginning sounds they hear in *branch* as you repeat the word several times. Ask students what color the branch of a tree is most of the time. (brown) Then ask if they hear the same beginning sounds in the word *brown*. Label the drawing by writing *brown branch*. Have a volunteer circle the two letters that spell the beginning sounds they hear in *branch* and *brown*. (br)

Repeat the procedure using the terms *fresh fruit* and the apples in the tree to demonstrate the *fr* consonant blend.

Challenge Words

front   bread   tramp
friend   treat

Have students close their books and write the missing word in the each sentence. When they have finished, have them check their words and spellings.

1. My dog Rags can act like a _____ without a home. (tramp)
2. Rags goes to my friend's _____ door. (front)
3. He barks for my _____ to come out. (friend)
4. Rags wants a _____ from him. (treat)
5. Rags will even eat _____! (bread)

Sentence Dictation Test

The vocabulary in these dictation sentences is within reach of most students at this level. You may have students write the entire sentence using invented spellings for words they are uncertain about or have students simply write the underlined spelling words.

Core Words

1. The <u>frisky</u> cat played.
2. A <u>frog</u> sat on the log.
3. I will <u>trade</u> with you.
4. Please sweep with the <u>broom</u>.
5. The pig wanted a <u>brick</u> home.
6. The stars are very <u>bright</u>.
7. I will <u>train</u> my dog.
8. The bus ride is <u>free</u>.
9. Did you see the <u>trick</u>?
10. It is not nice to <u>brag</u>.

Challenge Words

11. A boat ride is a <u>treat</u>.
12. Stand at the <u>front</u> of the room.
13. I want to bake <u>bread</u>.
14. Who is your best <u>friend</u>?
15. Do not <u>tramp</u> on the roses.

Answers to the Exercises

Focus
page 90
1–10. *br:* brag, brick, bright, broom
fr: free, frog, frisky
tr: train, trade, trick
11–15. ⓕⓡont, ⓑⓡead, ⓣⓡamp, ⓕⓡiend, ⓣⓡeat

Words and Meanings
page 91
1. frog
2. free
3. brag
4. bright
5. frisky
6. train
7. trick
8. brick
9. broom
10. trade

Word Works
11. train
12. bright
13. free
14. trade
15. trick

Word Play
page 92
1–5. brag, trade, frog, frisky, broom
6–7. brick, trick
8–9. free, broom
10. frisky
11. bright
12. broom
13. train
14. frog
15. brick

Write on Your Own
page 93
Stories will vary. Be sure students use three Core Words in their stories. Check for students' use of adjectives to describe their pets.

Proofreading Practice
1. bright
2. frisky
3. tricks
4. ...week.
5. ...tricks.

Spelling Words with *sl* and *sp*

Objectives
- to learn the spellings for the /sl/ and /sp/ consonant blends and apply them to both reading and writing
- to identify action words
- to learn and practice proofreading skills

Mini Lesson

Objective
- to discover the spellings for the /sl/ and /sp/ consonant blends

Ask students to name an animal that lives in a web. (spider) Draw a web on the chalkboard with a spider in it. Then ask students to listen carefully for the beginning sounds they hear as you repeat the word *spider* several times. Write the word *spider* in the web. Point to the letters as you say the word again. Ask a volunteer to circle the two letters that spell the beginning sounds they hear in *spider*.

Repeat the procedure for the *sl* blend using the word *slipper* and a drawing of a slipper.

Encourage students to suggest words they know with the same beginning sounds as *spider* and *slipper*. As the students say the words aloud, have them write the word under the correct picture on the chalkboard.

Challenge Words

spoon   slant   speak
spark   spoke

Have students close their books and write the Challenge Word that matches each of these clues. When they have finished, have them check their words and spellings.

1. *It has a short a sound. (slant)*
2. *It has a long e sound. (speak)*
3. *It has a long o sound. (spoke)*
4. *It has the same vowel sound as moon. (spoon)*
5. *It has a vowel + r sound. (spark)*

Sentence Dictation Test

The vocabulary in these dictation sentences is within reach of most students at this level. You may have students write the entire sentence using invented spellings for words they are uncertain about or have students simply write the underlined spelling words.

Core Words

1. The road was <u>slick</u>.
2. The bus gained <u>speed</u>.
3. Please do not <u>slam</u> the door.
4. A top will <u>spin</u>.
5. Take care not to <u>slip</u>.
6. The plants need <u>space</u>.
7. I keep my <u>sled</u> in the shed.
8. She made a <u>speech</u>.
9. The <u>slide</u> is wet.
10. The <u>spy</u> wore a shirt.

Challenge Words

11. Use a <u>spoon</u>.
12. A <u>spark</u> set the bush on fire.
13. The farmer <u>spoke</u> first.
14. Who will be first to <u>speak</u>?
15. The cart is parked on a <u>slant</u>.

Answers to the Exercises

Focus
page 94
1–5. slam, slip, slide, slick, sled
6–10. spin, speed, space, speech, spy
11–15. (sp)oon, (sl)ant, (sp)eak, (sp)ark, (sp)oke

Words and Meanings
page 95
1. sled
2. slide
3. speed
4. space
5. speech
6. slam
7. slick
8. slip
9. spin
10. spy

Word Works
11. talk
12. drive
13. smile
14. eat
15. sleep
16. share

Word Play
page 96
1–5. spin, spy, slide, speech, slip
6. Spin
7. Slide
8. Speed or Slip
9. Spy
10. slam
11. Slick
12. Speed
13. Sled
14. Space

Write on Your Own
page 97
Poems will vary. Be sure students use three Core Words in their poems. Check for use and spelling of rhyming words.

Proofreading Practice
1. slip
2. slide
3. space

Spelling Words Ending with -s

Objectives
- to learn the spellings of words that end with -s and apply them to both reading and writing
- to learn the plural form of some words
- to learn and practice proofreading skills

Mini Lesson

Objective
- to discover that most words add -s to make them mean more than one

Write the following words on one side of separate 3″ × 5″ cards and place them face down on a table or desk. Have several students take turns turning over one card at a time. Each time a matching singular and plural is revealed the student pronounces the two words and circles the letter that has been added to the plural.

| animal | animals | snake | snakes | ant | ants |
| duck | ducks | rabbit | rabbits | zebra | zebras |

Challenge Words

lions   *bears*   *tigers*
chipmunks   *kangaroos*

Have students close their books and write the Challenge Word that answers each riddle. When they have finished, have them check their words and spellings.

1. *They are large, have fur, and sleep during the winter.* (bears)
2. *They are large cats, live in the jungle, and have stripes.* (tigers)
3. *They hop around and mothers carry their babies in pockets.* (kangaroos)
4. *They are large cats and the males have long hair around their faces.* (lions)
5. *They are very small and have stripes down their backs.* (chipmunks)

Sentence Dictation Test

The vocabulary in these dictation sentences is within reach of most students at this level. You may have students write the entire sentence using invented spellings for words they are uncertain about or have students simply write the underlined spelling words.

Core Words

1. We milked the <u>cows</u>.
2. Blue <u>whales</u> are the biggest <u>animals</u>.
3. I fed the <u>ducks</u> and <u>chickens</u>.
4. The <u>rabbits</u> stay in the cage.
5. The <u>seals</u> dove into the pool.
6. Are the stripes on <u>zebras</u> black or white?
7. Many <u>ants</u> live in that hill of sand.
8. Do all <u>snakes</u> shed their skin?

Challenge Words

9. The <u>bears</u> will rest for a long time.
10. Can you train <u>chipmunks</u>?
11. We will see many <u>lions</u> and <u>tigers</u>.
12. Will <u>kangaroos</u> harm you?

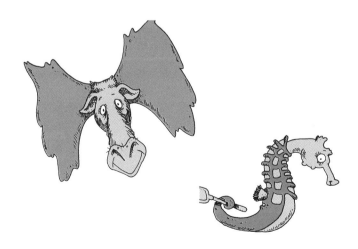

Focus
page 98
1–10. duck(s), cow(s), whale(s), seal(s), rabbit(s), ant(s), chicken(s), zebra(s), snake(s), animal(s)
11–15. lion(s), bear(s), tiger(s), chipmunk(s), kangaroo(s)

Words and Meanings
page 99
1. animals
2. chickens
3. ducks
4. cows
5. rabbits
6. ants
7. zebras
8. snakes
9. seals
10. whales

Word Works
11. highways
12. pizzas
13. combs
14. books
15. birds

Word Play
page 100
1. zebras
2. ants, snakes
3. ducks
4. chickens
5. ants
6. rabbits
7. whales
8. cows
9. seals
10. ants
11. chickens
12. zebras
13. snakes
14. ducks
15. rabbits
16. animals

Write on Your Own
page 101
Reports will vary. Be sure students use three Core Words in their reports. Check for inclusion of factual information about the animal chosen.

Proofreading Practice
1. animals
2. whales
3. seals
4. They live...
5. Some eat...

28 Spelling Words That Sound Alike

Objectives
- to learn the spellings for some common homophones and apply them to both reading and writing
- to learn abbreviations
- to learn and practice proofreading skills

Mini Lesson

Objective
- to discover the spellings for some common homophones

Ask students to listen carefully as you say the following sentence several times:

> **I see the sea.**

Ask which two words sound the same in the sentence. Ask if the two words mean the same thing. Repeat the sentence if necessary and ask what the first *see* means. Follow by asking what the second *sea* means.

Put each of this lesson's words on a separate 3" 3 5" card. Allow students to pick a card without seeing the word on the card. Call on a student to read her word and use it in a sentence. Then the student with the homophone for that word does the same. Let the class decide if the words have been used correctly.

Challenge Words

seam   seem   eye
too   to

Have students close their books and write the missing Challenge Words in the sentences. When they have finished, have them check their words and spellings.

1. I have something in my _____. (eye)
2. The grapes are _____ ripe. (too)
3. I _____ to have lost my pencil. (seem)
4. I need _____ study tonight. (to)
5. Jack ripped the _____ of his shirt. (seam)

Sentence Dictation Test

The vocabulary in these dictation sentences is within reach of most students at this level. You may have students write the entire sentence using invented spellings for words they are uncertain about or have students simply write the underlined spelling words.

Core Words

1. We ate the <u>meat</u>.
2. I want to <u>dye</u> my dress.
3. The <u>deer</u> ran fast.
4. My class <u>rode</u> on the bus.
5. Whales live in the <u>sea</u>.
6. We plan to <u>meet</u> in the park.
7. Why did the fish <u>die</u>?
8. The <u>road</u> has many bumps.
9. Can you <u>see</u> the moon?
10. You are a <u>dear</u> friend.

Challenge Words

11. The speech was <u>too</u> long.
12. I had dust in my <u>eye</u>.
13. Does the frog <u>seem</u> frisky?
14. The animals went <u>to</u> the barn.
15. I ripped the <u>seam</u> of my dress.

Focus
page 102
1–10. see, sea, dear, deer, meet, meat, road, rode, dye, die
11–15. seam, seem, (eye), too, to

Words and Meanings
page 103
1. dear
2. rode
3. see
4. deer
5. road
6. die
7. sea
8. dye
9. meet
10. meat

Word Works
11. Doctor, Dr.
12. Mister, Mr.
13. Street, St.
14. Avenue, Ave.
15. November, Nov.

Word Play
page 104
1. see
2. sea
3. road
4. rode
5. dear
6. deer
7. meat
8. meet
9. die
10. dye
11. road
12. rode
13. deer
14. dear
15. meat
16. meet
17. sea
18. see
19. die
20. dye

Write on Your Own
page 105
Letters will vary. Be sure students use four Core Words in their letters. Check for inclusion of the parts of a friendly letter.

Proofreading Practice
1. dear
2. road
3. meet
4. see

Spelling Family Names

Objectives
- to learn the spellings for family names and apply them to both reading and writing
- to learn four common personal pronouns
- to learn and practice proofreading skills

Mini Lesson

Objective
- to discover familiar spelling patterns in the spellings for family names

Write the word *family* on the chalkboard. Above it write father and mother and gradually build a family tree like the one below by asking students on which line each word in the spelling list belongs.

> *grandfather - grandmother*
> *uncle - father - mother - aunt*
> *brother - sister - baby*
> *family*

Say each word slowly for students and challenge them to find some sounds and spellings they have studied. Here are some possible discoveries:

- *family* has the short *a* sound spelled *a* as in *man* and *hat*.
- *mother-father*, and *brother* have the /th/ sound spelled *th* as in *this* and *that*.
- *sister* has the short *i* sound spelled *i* as in *pin* and *fix*.
- *grandmother* and *grandfather* have the *-nd* consonant blend found in *sand* and *pond*.
- *uncle* has the short *u* sound spelled *u* as in *us* and *mud*.

Challenge Words

parent   children   together
person   twins

Have students close their books and write the missing word in each sentence. When they have finished, have them check their words and spellings.

1. *Animals* is to *animal* as *people* is to _____. (person)
2. *Son* is to *child* as *mother* is to _____. (parent)
3. *Three* is to *triplets* as *two* is to _____. (twins)
4. *Big* is to *little* as *apart* is to _____. (together)
5. *Woman* is to *women* as *child* is to _____. (children)

Sentence Dictation Test

The vocabulary in these dictation sentences is within reach of most students at this level. You may have students write the entire sentence using invented spellings for words they are uncertain about or have students simply write the underlined spelling words.

Core Words

1. My <u>sister</u> goes to school.
2. The <u>baby</u> is taking a nap.
3. I helped my <u>father</u>.
4. My <u>mother</u> is a teacher.
5. My <u>grandmother</u> jogs every day.
6. Does your <u>grandfather</u> like to fish?
7. I went to the zoo with my <u>uncle</u>.
8. His <u>aunt</u> can ride a horse.
9. That <u>family</u> lives on a farm.
10. Her <u>brother</u> is in my class.

Challenge Words

11. The animals live <u>together</u> in the barn.
12. A note was sent to every <u>parent</u>.
13. The <u>children</u> rode on the train.
14. We met the <u>person</u> who gave the speech.
15. I saw the <u>twins</u> at camp.

Answers to the Exercises

Focus
page 106
1–6. mother, sister, grandmother, grandfather, father, brother
7–8. family, baby
9–10. aunt, uncle
11–15. parent, children, together, person, twins

Words and Meanings
page 107
1. family
2. mother
3. father
4. baby
5. brother
6. sister
7. aunt
8. grandmother
9. uncle
10. grandfather

Word Works
11. She will sing.
12. We can go.
13. They ski.
14. He works at home.
15. She has a cat.

Word Play
page 108
1. sister
2. brother
3. mother
4. father
5. aunt
6. uncle
7. grandmother
8. grandfather
9. aunt
10. uncle
11. grandmother
12. grandfather
13. brother
14. sister
15. family
16. baby

Write on Your Own
page 109
Descriptions will vary. Be sure students use three Core Words in their descriptions. Check for use of adjectives and adverbs students use to describe the person chosen.

Proofreading Practice
1. aunt
2. family
3. brother
4. sister
5. ...special?

30 Review

Objectives
- to recall and spell representative Core and Challenge Words from Lessons 25–29
- to demonstrate a knowledge of words and spelling principles in standardized testing formats

Challenge Words Game

Objective
- to review spelling patterns in Lessons 25–29

The following game can be played with the entire class or with selected students. Another strategy is to divide students into two teams and play the game competitively.

The object of the game is to be the first student or team to identify a Challenge Word and spell it correctly from a series of clues that you read one at a time.

If a student or team is the first to call out the word and write it correctly on the chalkboard, that student or team is awarded 2 points.

If another student or team challenges the word or the spelling and corrects the error, that student or team is awarded 5 points. However, if they challenge the word or the spelling, and the word is correct, that student or team loses 2 points.

Here are some possible words and their clues. You may wish to create additional ones. You might also have students make up a set of clues to try on the class.

Challenge Words and Clues

kangaroos

1. It begins with a *k* and has the vowel sound you hear in *blue*.
2. They have pockets but don't wear clothes.
3. It is an odd-looking animal.
4. The first syllable rhymes with *sang*.
5. Most live in Australia.

spoon

1. It is made out of wood, plastic, or metal and has a handle.
2. It begins with two consonants.
3. The /ü/ sound is spelled *oo*.
4. It rhymes with *moon*.
5. You use it to eat cereal or soup.

bread

1. It begins with the same consonant sounds as *brown*.
2. The short *e* sound is spelled *ea*.
3. You need it to make a sandwich.
4. It rhymes with *sled*.
5. It usually comes in loaves.

Sentence Dictation Test

Each sentence below contains a spelling word studied in this Review Lesson. You may wish to have students write the entire sentence using invented spellings for the other words in the sentence or have students write only the underlined words.

Core Words

1. Two <u>ducks</u> swam across the lake.
2. I can <u>see</u> them from my room.
3. The mayor <u>rode</u> in the parade.
4. His <u>brother</u> plays football.
5. My sister has a pet <u>frog</u>.
6. She let me use her <u>sled</u>.
7. The story was about a <u>spy</u>.
8. Use a <u>broom</u> to clean the floor.
9. We hear a <u>train</u> whistle.
10. The wind made the blades <u>spin</u>.
11. The crumbs were eaten by <u>ants</u>.
12. We must try to save the <u>whales</u>.
13. The man used a blue <u>dye</u> to color the water.
14. My <u>uncle</u> took a trip.
15. The teacher asked my <u>father</u> to help.

Challenge Words

16. She is my best <u>friend</u>.
17. The fire was started by a <u>spark</u>.
18. The class watched the <u>chipmunks</u> play in the tree.
19. I hope you can come to the party <u>too</u>.
20. Let's walk to the beach <u>together</u>.

Additional Assessment

Standardized-format Test

This Review Lesson may also be evaluated using the black-line master test in a standardized test format on page T100.

Words from Reading and Writing

You may wish to have students exchange their lists of words from reading and writing on the Home Study Words form and test each other.

Crossword Puzzle

For additional practice with the words from the previous five lessons, have students complete the crossword puzzle that appears as a black-line master on page T94.

31 Spelling the /ủ/ Sound

Objectives
- to learn two spellings for the /ủ/ sound and apply them to both reading and writing
- to learn unusual plurals
- to learn and practice proofreading skills

Mini Lesson

Objective
- to discover two spellings for the /ủ/ sound

Ask students to name words that describe your actions as you push and pull a book across a table. (push, pull) Have students listen carefully for the vowel sound as you say each word several times. Then ask them to listen as you repeat the word *book* several times. Ask them if they hear the same vowel sound in *book.* (yes)

Write *book* and *push* on the chalkboard. Ask students if they hear the vowel sound at the beginning, middle, or end of the word. Follow up by having students volunteer to underline the letter or letters in the two words that spell the vowel sound.

Read the words below one at a time and ask a volunteer to write the word correctly under *book* if the vowel is spelled *oo,* or under *push* if the vowel is spelled *u.* When all words have been written, check the spellings in the lesson word list.

| hook | full | good | foot | put | push |

Challenge Words

crook *stood* *shook*
wool *cookbook*

Have students close their books and write the Challenge Word that matches each clue.

1. It is what some sweaters are made of. (wool)
2. It is what the wind did to the trees. (shook)
3. This word rhymes with *hook.* (crook)
4. This book tells how to cook. (cookbook)
5. This is what people did when they got up to leave. (stood)

Sentence Dictation Test

The vocabulary in these dictation sentences is within reach of most students at this level. You may have students write the entire sentence using invented spellings for words they are uncertain about or have students simply write the underlined spelling words.

Core Words

1. The horse will <u>pull</u> the cart.
2. Who <u>took</u> you to the zoo?
3. Where is my <u>book</u>?
4. Rain is <u>good</u> for the plants.
5. I <u>put</u> the bricks in the box.
6. We saw the <u>full</u> moon.
7. Did you <u>look</u> in the barn?
8. The tip of a <u>hook</u> is very sharp.
9. My right <u>foot</u> is sore.
10. Please help me <u>push</u> the sled.

Challenge Words

11. The kitten slept in the <u>crook</u> of my arm.
12. We <u>stood</u> at the back of the room.
13. My pants are made of <u>wool</u>.
14. The crash <u>shook</u> the barn.
15. Your <u>cookbook</u> is on the shelf.

Answers to the Exercises

Focus
page 112
1–10. p(u)t, h(oo)k, f(u)ll, t(oo)k, p(u)sh, f(oo)t, b(oo)k, p(u)ll, l(oo)k, g(oo)d
11–15. cr(oo)k, st(oo)d, sh(oo)k, w(oo)l, c(oo)kb(oo)k

Words and Meanings
page 113
1. look
2. book
3. full
4. good
5. took
6. hook
7. put
8. foot
9. pull
10. push

Word Works
11. feet
12. men
13. women
14. children
15. mice
16. geese

Word Play
page 114
1–4. hook, took, book, look
5. good
6. took
7. full
8. pull
9. book
10. hook
11. look
12. push
13. put
14. foot

Write on Your Own
page 115
Books reports will vary. Students should use three Core Words in their reports. Check for capitalization of the book title and inclusion of an opinion about the book.

Proofreading Practice
1–3. book, good, put

32 Spelling Words Ending in -*ed* and -*ing*

Objectives
- to learn to double the final consonant of some words before adding -*ed* or -*ing*
- to form words with long vowel sounds
- to learn and practice dictionary and proofreading skills

Mini Lesson

Objective
- to discover that some words double the final consonant before adding -*ed* or -*ing*

Write the following sentence on the chalkboard and ask students to supply the missing word.

> Today I will tap on the door. Yesterday I _____ on the door. (tapped)

Write the word *tapped* on the blank. Ask students the difference in the meaning of "today I tap" and "Yesterday I tapped." (The second sentence tells about something in the past.) Ask how the spelling of *tap* changed when the -*ed* was added. (the final consonant was doubled) Write the following two words on the chalkboard.

> tapped   taped

Ask students if these two words mean the same thing? (no) Would the sentence on the chalkboard mean the same thing if *taped* were used instead of *tapped*? Conclude by asking students if they think it is important to double the last consonant before adding some endings. (yes)

Challenge Words

running   skipping   digging
hopping   begged

Have students close their books and write the Challenge Words that complete each sentence.

1. Dan was _____ a hole. (digging)
2. Rita was _____ a race. (running)
3. Sandy was _____ rope. (skipping)
4. Hal was _____ on one foot. (hopping)
5. Only our dog _____ for something to eat. (begged)

Sentence Dictation Test

The vocabulary in these dictation sentences is within reach of most students at this level. You may have students write the entire sentence using invented spellings for words they are uncertain about or have students simply write the underlined spelling words.

Core Words

1. We had to <u>mop</u> up the mess.
2. I <u>cut</u> my hand on the blade.
3. Who <u>mopped</u> the tiles?
4. The grass needs <u>cutting</u>.
5. Can you <u>hit</u> the ball over the net?
6. I keep <u>hitting</u> my toe on that rock.
7. Which bird <u>tapped</u> at the tree?
8. Can you swing the <u>bat</u>?
9. Use a hammer to <u>tap</u> the nail.
10. Who is <u>batting</u> last?

Challenge Words

11. A rabbit is <u>hopping</u> in the yard.
12. I am <u>digging</u> a hole in the sand.
13. The dogs <u>begged</u> for more bones.
14. Who is <u>running</u> in the race?
15. Try <u>skipping</u> a flat stone.

Answers to the Exercises

Focus
page 116
1–10. mop, mo(pp)ed, hit, hi(tt)ing, bat, ba(tt)ing, tap, ta(pp)ed, cut, cu(tt)ing
11–15. ru(nn)ing, ski(pp)ing, di(gg)ing, ho(pp)ing, be(gg)ed

Words and Meanings
page 117
1. tapped
2. bat
3. mopped
4. hitting or batting
5. batting or hitting
6. cutting
7. cut
8. tap
9. mop
10. hit

Word Works
11. cane
12. pine
13. tube
14. robe
15. hope
16. made

Word Play
page 118
1. bat
2. cut
3. mop
4. tap
5. hit
6–8. hit, bat, cut
9–11. hitting, batting, cutting
12–13. mop, tap
14–15. mopped, tapped
16–18. hitting, batting, cutting
19. bats, batted, batting
20. mops, mopped, mopping
21. cut, cutting
22. hit, hitting
23. tapped, tapping
24. teeth

Write on Your Own
page 119
Newspaper stories will vary. Students should use three Core Words in their stories. Check for logical order of sentences.

Proofreading Practice
1–3. bat, hit, hitting

33 Spelling the /ou/ Sound

Objectives
- to learn two spellings for the /ou/ sound and apply them to both reading and writing
- to identify words that tell *when*
- to learn and practice proofreading skills

Mini Lesson

Objective
- to discover two spellings for the /ou/ sound

Draw the outline of a house and an owl on the chalkboard. Ask students to listen carefully for the vowel sound they hear in each word as you pronounce the words several times. Ask if they hear the same vowel sound. (yes) Write *house* and *owl* on the appropriate picture. Ask students which letters spell the vowel sound in each word and underline the letters. (ho<u>use</u>, <u>ow</u>l)

Tell them you will read a list of words to them. Ask them to raise their hands if they hear the same vowel sound they hear in *house* and *owl.* When they hear such a word, ask for a volunteer to try to spell the word on the chalkboard, writing it in the house or the owl depending on the spelling.

> now look out talk loud sound tap clown our hit down owl town

Conclude by having students check their spellings with the lesson word list.

Challenge Words

found   howl   south
crown   around

Have students close their books and write the Challenge Word that fits each clue.

1. *not north, east, or west (south)*
2. *the way a merry-go-round goes (around)*
3. *not lost anymore (found)*
4. *the thing a king and queen wear on their heads (crown)*
5. *the sound a wolf makes (howl)*

Sentence Dictation Test

The vocabulary in these dictation sentences is within reach of most students at this level. You may have students write the entire sentence using invented spellings for words they are uncertain about or have students simply write the underlined spelling words.

Core Words

1. The <u>clown</u> did a trick.
2. I will read a book <u>now</u>.
3. An <u>owl</u> lives in that tree.
4. A <u>loud</u> <u>sound</u> woke us up.
5. We took the bus to <u>town</u>.
6. Please come to <u>our</u> <u>house</u>.
7. Put your foot <u>down</u>.
8. The batter struck <u>out</u>.

Challenge Words

9. We <u>found</u> a <u>crown</u>.
10. Birds fly <u>south</u> in the winter.
11. Why did the child <u>howl</u>?
12. I rode <u>around</u> the lake.

Answers to the Exercises

Focus
page 120
1–10. (ou)t, n(ow), cl(ow)n, (ou)r, d(ow)n, s(ou)nd, (ow)l, h(ou)se, t(ow)n, l(ou)d
11–15. f(ou)nd, h(ow)l, s(ou)th, cr(ow)n, ar(ou)nd

Words and Meanings
page 121
1. town
2. house
3. now
4. clown
5. out
6. down
7. sound
8. loud
9. our
10. owl

Word Works
11. today
12. never
13. always
14. sometimes
15. tomorrow
16. yesterday

Word Play
page 122
1. out
2. now
3. sound
4. our
5. loud
6. owl
7. house
8–10. clown, down, town
11. sound
12. clown
13. owl
14. house
15. now
16. Town
17. Loud
18. Out

Write on Your Own
page 123
Lists will vary. Students should use three Core Words in their lists. Check for a complete thought in each list item.

Proofreading Practice
1–3. sound, clown, owl

34 Spelling Compound Words

Objectives
- to learn the spellings of compound words and apply them to both reading and writing
- to identify words that tell *where*
- to learn and practice proofreading skills

Mini Lesson

Objective
- to discover the spellings of compound words

Write compound words from the lesson or other compound words on pieces of construction paper or index cards. Use scissors to carefully cut each card into two parts between the two words that make up the compound word. Make each cut irregular like a puzzle piece. Distribute the cut cards randomly to students. Then allow them to move about the class trying to find the match for their part. After the match, ask each pair of students to report on the two words that they put together to form another word and write the compound word on the chalkboard. The activity can be repeated using words students suggest.

Challenge Words

sailboat   downtown   weekend   everywhere   sandbox

Have students write the Challenge Words that mean the following.

1. a boat that sails (sailboat)
2. a box of sand (sandbox)
3. the end of the week (weekend)
4. in all places (everywhere)
5. the main part of a town (downtown)

Sentence Dictation Test

The vocabulary in these dictation sentences is within reach of most students at this level. You may have students write the entire sentence using invented spellings for words they are uncertain about or have students simply write the underlined spelling words.

Core Words

1. Where did you put the <u>notebook</u>?
2. The animals went <u>into</u> the barn.
3. We painted the <u>doghouse</u>.
4. The rabbit held <u>something</u> in its teeth.
5. My <u>bedroom</u> is very small.
6. The <u>lunchroom</u> was full.
7. <u>Maybe</u> you can help me rake.
8. I washed the dishes and <u>nobody</u> helped me.
9. I did it <u>myself</u>.
10. They went <u>inside</u> after lunch.

Challenge Words

11. We went in our <u>sailboat</u>.
12. My pal and I went to the zoo last <u>weekend</u>.
13. I like to shop <u>downtown</u>.
14. Nobody plays in the <u>sandbox</u>.
15. I go <u>everywhere</u> by bike.

Answers to the Exercises

Focus
page 124
1–10. (may)(be), (bed)(room), (lunch)(room), (in)(to), (some)(thing), (no)(body), (dog)(house), (my)(self), (in)(side), (note)(book)
11–15. (sail)(boat), (down)(town), (week)(end), (every)(where), (sand)(box)

Words and Meanings
page 125
1. nobody
2. bedroom
3. myself
4. something
5. maybe
6. doghouse
7. inside
8. notebook
9. into
10. lunchroom

Word Works
11. out
12. below
13. down
14. upstairs
15. around
16. across

Word Play
page 126
1–5. maybe, something, myself, inside, notebook
6. lunchroom
7. notebook
8. maybe
9. doghouse
10. bedroom
11. nobody
12. into

Write on Your Own
page 127
Descriptions will vary. Students should use three Core Words in their descriptions. Use this activity to discuss changes that have taken place this year.

Proofreading Practice
1–3. myself, lunchroom, notebook
4–5. ...recess. ...lunchroom.

Spelling Number Words

Objectives
- to learn the spellings of number words and apply them to both reading and writing
- to choose the correct homophones for number words
- to learn and practice proofreading skills

Mini Lesson

Objective
- to discover the spellings of number words

Ask a volunteer to write the numerals from one to ten in a column on the chalkboard. Have volunteers take turns writing a number word beside each numeral. If students have difficulty spelling any of the words, allow them to invent the spelling. When all the appropriate words have been written, check the spelling of the words with the lesson word list.

After the spelling has been checked, ask students to identify the number word or words that fit each of these clues:

- Two words that have a long *i* sound spelled *i-e* (five; nine)
- This word starts with the same sound as *worm,* but does not have the letter *w* (one)
- This word ends with the long *e* sound spelled *ee* (three)
- This word spells the long *a* sound *eigh* (eight)
- Two words that have the short *e* sound spelled *e* (ten; seven)

Allow students to make up clues to use with classmates.

Challenge Words

count   add   numbers
minus   second

Have students close their books and write the missing Challenge Word in each sentence.

1. I am the _____ person in line. (second)
2. One and two are _____. (numbers)
3. Six _____ four is two. (minus)
4. Close your eyes and _____ to 100. (count)
5. Can you _____ three and six? (add)

Sentence Dictation Test

The vocabulary in these dictation sentences is within reach of most students at this level. You may have students write the entire sentence using invented spellings for words they are uncertain about or have students simply write the underlined spelling words.

Core Words

1. Those <u>two</u> dogs chased the cat.
2. My family has <u>four</u> bikes.
3. We planted <u>eight</u> trees.
4. The hen laid <u>one</u> egg.
5. The team has <u>nine</u> players.
6. I have <u>three</u> uncles.
7. The band played <u>ten</u> songs.
8. Can <u>five</u> of us sleep in the tent?
9. The zoo has <u>six</u> seals.
10. We will read <u>seven</u> books.

Challenge Words

11. Can you <u>count</u> to ten?
12. I came in <u>second</u> in the race.
13. What is seven <u>minus</u> five?
14. Print the <u>numbers</u>.
15. Can you <u>add</u> ten and nine?

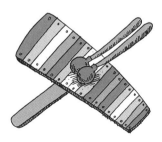

Answers to the Exercises

Focus
page 128
1–10. (o)ne, two, thr(ee), four, f(i)v(e), s(i)x, s(e)ven, (eigh)t, n(i)n(e), t(e)n
11–15. count, add, numbers, minus, second (*Ringed answers may vary.*)

Words and Meanings
page 129
1. seven
2. eight
3. two
4. one
5. ten
6. five
7. four
8. three
9. six
10. nine

Word Works
11. to
12. one
13. ate
14. four

Word Play
page 130
1. three
2. two
3. four
4. six
5. one
6. seven
7. five
8. ten
9. two
10. three
11. one
12. four
13. seven
14. nine
15. eight

Write on Your Own
page 131
Stories will vary. Students should use three Core Words in their stories. Check for choice and organization of physical or mental self descriptions.

Proofreading Practice
1–3. seven, four, one

Review

Objectives
- to recall and spell representative Core and Challenge Words from Lessons 31–35
- to demonstrate a knowledge of words and spelling principles in standardized testing formats

Challenge Words Game

Objective
- to review spelling patterns in Lessons 31–35

The following game can be played with the entire class or with selected students. Another strategy is to divide students into two teams and play the game competitively.

The object of the game is to be the first student or team to identify a Challenge Word and spell it correctly from a series of clues that you read one at a time.

If a student or team is the first to call out the word and write it correctly on the chalkboard, that student or team is awarded 2 points.

If another student or team challenges the word or the spelling and corrects the error, that student or team is awarded 5 points. However, if they challenge the word or the spelling, and the word is correct, that student or team loses 2 points.

Here are some possible words and their clues. You may wish to create additional ones. You might also have students make up a set of clues to try on the class.

Challenge Words and Clues

cookbook	crown	weekend
1. This is usually found in the kitchen.	1. It begins with the letter *c* spelling the /k/ sound.	1. It starts on Friday night.
2. It is a word made out of two shorter words.	2. It has the /ou/ sound spelled *ow*.	2. It is made up of two smaller words.
3. The vowel sound you hear in *put* appears twice in the word.	3. It rhymes with *down*.	3. It has a long e and a short e sound.
4. The syllables rhyme with each other.	4. This is something a queen would wear.	4. It ends with the same two consonants as *pond*.
5. This is a collection of recipes.	5. It is worn on the head.	5. It describes a period of time.

Sentence Dictation Test

Each sentence below contains a spelling word studied in this Review Lesson. You may wish to have students write the entire sentence using invented spellings for the other words in the sentence or have students write only the underlined words.

Core Words

1. Three plus one makes <u>four</u>.
2. There are <u>two</u> sides to every story.
3. Do not forget your <u>notebook</u>.
4. That <u>owl</u> has not moved all day.
5. My <u>house</u> is in the next block.
6. Someone has <u>mopped</u> the floor.
7. Take a <u>book</u> with you on the trip.
8. Try to do a <u>good</u> deed each day.
9. There were <u>eight</u> pens on the desk.
10. <u>Maybe</u> we will see him there.
11. We stood in line in the <u>lunchroom</u>.
12. Be careful when you go <u>down</u> the stairs.
13. I gently <u>tapped</u> on the door.
14. Give the swing a hard <u>push</u>.
15. She is <u>batting</u> for the team.

Challenge Words

16. My gloves are made out of <u>wool</u>.
17. The rabbit was seen <u>hopping</u> away.
18. He lives on the <u>south</u> side of town.
19. The sound could be heard <u>everywhere</u>.
20. You must read the <u>numbers</u> on the sign.

Additional Assessment

Standardized-format Test

This review lesson may also be evaluated using the black-line master test in a standardized test format on page T101.

Words from Reading and Writing

You may wish to have students exchange their lists of words from reading and writing on the Home Study Words form and test each other.

Crossword Puzzle

For additional practice with the words from the previous five lessons, have students complete the crossword puzzle that appears as a black-line master on page T95.

SRA Spelling Word List Grade 2

Lesson	List	Word	Lesson	List	Word	Lesson	List	Word	Lesson	List	Word
35	CH	add	27	CR	chickens	23	CR	every	21	CR	hard
21	CH	alarm	20	CH	child	34	CH	everywhere	21	CH	harm
5	CR	and	29	CH	children	28	CH	eye	1	CR	has
27	CR	animals	27	CH	chipmunks	29	CR	family	1	CR	hat
27	CR	ants	20	CR	choke	21	CR	farm	13	CR	hay
23	CR	any	20	CH	chore	5	CR	fast	2	CR	hid
21	CH	arm	19	CR	clash	1	CR	fat	2	CR	his
33	CH	around	4	CH	click	29	CR	father	32	CR	hit
21	CR	art	4	CH	clock	7	CR	fed	32	CR	hitting
1	CH	as	33	CR	clown	15	CR	fight	31	CR	hook
11	CR	ask	16	CH	coach	22	CR	first	32	CH	hopping
29	CR	aunt	16	CR	coat	2	CH	fish	22	CR	horn
23	CH	away	31	CH	cookbook	35	CR	five	22	CR	horse
29	CR	baby	3	CH	cot	2	CR	fix	33	CR	house
4	CH	backpack	35	CH	count	19	CR	flash	33	CH	howl
1	CR	bad	27	CR	cows	16	CH	float	8	CH	hush
13	CR	bait	14	CH	cream	4	CH	flock	2	CR	if
17	CH	balloon	31	CH	crook	3	CR	flop	34	CR	inside
5	CR	band	3	CH	cross	15	CR	fly	34	CR	into
21	CR	barn	33	CH	crown	3	CR	fog	1	CH	jam
32	CR	bat	15	CR	cry	17	CR	food	3	CR	job
20	CR	bath	32	CR	cut	31	CR	foot	3	CR	jog
32	CR	batting	17	CH	cute	22	CR	for	11	CR	jump
27	CH	bears	32	CR	cutting	33	CH	found	5	CR	just
34	CR	bedroom	21	CR	dark	35	CR	four	27	CH	kangaroos
32	CH	begged	1	CH	dash	25	CR	free	4	CR	kick
7	CR	bend	28	CR	dear	25	CH	friend	23	CH	kind
22	CR	bird	14	CR	deep	25	CR	frisky	2	CR	kiss
10	CH	blank	28	CR	deer	25	CR	frog	5	CH	land
10	CH	blanket	11	CR	desk	25	CH	front	1	CR	lap
10	CR	blast	28	CR	die	31	CR	full	5	CR	last
13	CH	blaze	32	CH	digging	1	CR	gas	14	CH	leave
10	CR	blend	22	CH	dinosaur	22	CR	girl	15	CR	light
11	CH	blimp	22	CR	dirt	23	CR	give	27	CH	lions
10	CR	blink	2	CH	dish	10	CR	glad	5	CR	list
10	CR	block	4	CR	dock	10	CR	glass	23	CR	live
16	CR	blow	23	CR	does	16	CH	globe	4	CR	lock
16	CR	boat	3	CR	dog	10	CH	gloves	3	CR	log
31	CR	book	34	CR	doghouse	10	CH	glue	11	CR	long
17	CR	boot	33	CR	down	16	CR	goat	31	CR	look
23	CH	both	34	CH	downtown	23	CH	goes	5	CR	lost
25	CR	brag	14	CR	dream	23	CR	gone	3	CR	lot
25	CH	bread	9	CH	dress	31	CR	good	33	CR	loud
25	CR	brick	9	CR	drip	17	CH	goose	8	CR	luck
25	CR	bright	9	CR	drive	3	CR	got	8	CH	lunch
11	CH	bring	9	CR	drove	9	CR	grade	34	CR	lunchroom
25	CR	broom	9	CR	drum	9	CR	grand	1	CR	mad
29	CR	brother	15	CR	dry	29	CR	grandfather	1	CR	man
8	CH	bunch	27	CR	ducks	29	CR	grandmother	23	CH	many
13	CR	came	11	CR	dump	13	CR	grape	1	CR	map
11	CR	camp	8	CH	dust	9	CH	grass	21	CH	march
13	CR	cane	28	CR	dye	9	CR	grin	11	CR	mask
21	CR	cart	14	CR	each	9	CH	grow	34	CR	maybe
1	CH	cash	7	CR	egg	11	CH	grump	14	CR	meal
5	CH	cast	35	CR	eight	5	CR	hand	14	CH	mean

CR - Core Word   CH - Challenge Word

Lesson	List	Word	Lesson	List	Word	Lesson	List	Word	Lesson	List	Word
28	CR	meat	13	CR	rake	26	CR	slick	15	CH	tight
28	CR	meet	20	CH	reach	26	CR	slide	2	CR	tip
7	CH	mend	14	CR	read	26	CR	slip	28	CH	to
7	CH	mess	7	CR	rest	3	CH	slot	16	CR	toad
7	CR	met	2	CH	rich	16	CH	slow	16	CH	toast
15	CH	might	15	CR	right	15	CH	sly	29	CH	together
2	CR	milk	2	CR	rip	21	CH	smart	28	CH	too
35	CH	minus	28	CR	road	4	CR	snack	31	CR	took
2	CH	mitt	3	CH	robin	27	CR	snakes	20	CR	tooth
2	CR	mix	4	CR	rock	14	CH	sneeze	33	CR	town
17	CR	moon	28	CR	rode	16	CR	snow	25	CR	trade
17	CH	moose	17	CR	room	16	CR	soap	13	CH	trail
32	CR	mop	16	CR	row	3	CH	soggy	25	CR	train
32	CR	mopped	8	CR	rub	34	CR	something	25	CH	tramp
22	CR	more	17	CR	rude	11	CR	song	13	CH	tray
22	CH	morning	8	CR	rug	17	CR	soon	14	CR	treat
29	CR	mother	32	CH	running	33	CR	sound	25	CH	treat
20	CR	much	8	CH	rush	33	CH	south	9	CR	tree
8	CR	mud	8	CR	rust	26	CR	space	25	CR	trick
8	CR	must	4	CR	sack	26	CH	spark	9	CH	trim
34	CR	myself	34	CH	sailboat	26	CH	speak	9	CR	trip
15	CR	night	5	CR	sand	26	CR	speech	9	CR	truck
35	CR	nine	34	CH	sandbox	26	CR	speed	9	CH	try
34	CR	nobody	13	CR	say	26	CR	spin	17	CR	tube
16	CR	nose	28	CR	sea	26	CH	spoke	8	CR	tug
34	CR	notebook	27	CR	seals	26	CH	spoon	17	CR	tune
33	CR	now	28	CH	seam	3	CR	spot	29	CH	twins
35	CH	numbers	35	CH	second	26	CR	spy	35	CR	two
3	CR	off	28	CR	see	4	CR	stack	29	CR	uncle
35	CR	one	28	CH	seem	13	CH	stain	8	CR	us
33	CR	our	14	CR	seen	11	CH	stamp	23	CR	very
33	CR	out	7	CR	send	5	CH	stand	34	CH	weekend
33	CR	owl	35	CR	seven	21	CR	start	7	CR	went
4	CR	pack	4	CH	shack	7	CH	stem	23	CR	were
13	CR	pail	19	CH	shadow	4	CR	stick	7	CH	west
13	CH	pain	19	CH	shall	11	CR	sting	27	CH	whales
29	CH	parent	19	CR	shame	31	CH	stood	19	CR	what
21	CR	park	19	CH	share	22	CH	store	14	CR	wheel
5	CH	past	21	CR	sharp	15	CH	stripe	19	CR	where
1	CR	pat	14	CR	sheep	8	CR	stuck	19	CR	while
1	CH	path	19	CR	shine	20	CR	such	22	CH	whirl
7	CH	pen	22	CR	shirt	32	CR	tap	19	CH	whiskers
29	CH	person	19	CR	shock	32	CR	tapped	19	CH	whisper
2	CR	pin	31	CH	shook	11	CH	task	23	CR	who
15	CR	pine	17	CH	shoot	20	CR	teach	19	CR	why
10	CR	plan	19	CR	shore	14	CR	team	15	CR	wide
10	CH	planet	22	CR	short	35	CR	ten	5	CH	wind
13	CR	plate	8	CR	shut	7	CR	test	11	CR	wing
10	CR	plot	15	CH	shy	20	CR	thank	2	CH	wish
10	CR	plum	4	CR	sick	7	CR	them	20	CR	with
10	CR	plus	15	CR	sight	20	CH	thick	31	CH	wool
5	CR	pond	29	CR	sister	20	CR	thin	21	CR	yard
17	CR	pool	35	CR	six	20	CR	thing	7	CR	yet
31	CR	pull	32	CH	skipping	20	CH	think	23	CR	your
31	CR	push	26	CR	slam	22	CH	third	27	CR	zebras
31	CR	put	26	CH	slant	16	CR	those	17	CR	zoo
27	CR	rabbits	26	CR	sled	35	CR	three			
13	CR	raise	14	CH	sleep	27	CH	tigers			

CR - Core Word   CH - Challenge Word

Using the Mini Lessons with Invented Spelling

By observing the invented spellings that occur in student writing, you can identify patterns of misspelling and address them directly at the most teachable moment in the revising and proofreading stage of writing. In addition to providing an engaging and meaningful introduction to the lessons, the Mini Lessons in this Teacher's Edition can serve as brief lessons for those teachable moments whenever they occur.

The following chart of sample words and typical invented spellings will assist you in selecting appropriate Mini Lessons. It is not necessary that these exact misspellings occur in the writing sample. An analogous word and invented spelling serves equally well as an indicator.

Sample Word	Invented Spelling	Suggested Mini Lesson Level/Lesson
afraid	afaid	2/9, 2/10, 2/25, 2/26, 5/13
beat	bet	1/27, 2/14, 3/4, 4/2, 6/2
begged	bagd	2/32, 3/15, 4/15, 5/19
blow	blo	2/16
blue	blu	2/17, 3/5, 4/5, 5/9
boat	bot	2/16, 3/3, 3/4, 5/8
cat	cet	1/17, 2/1, 3/1
catch	cach	3/33, 4/13
chop	cop	1/32, 2/20, 4/13
circle	circal	3/11, 4/25, 5/15, 5/26
cliff	clif	3/10
	cif	1/22
climbing	climing	3/33, 4/29, 5/31, 6/13
doctor	docter	4/7, 4/17, 4/25, 5/26
face	fase	3/19, 4/10, 4/16, 6/5
field	feild	5/7
foot	fut	2/31
girl	gurl	2/22, 3/31, 4/19
girl's	girls	5/22
guess	gess	3/33, 4/29, 5/31, 6/13
having	haveing	3/13, 4/35

Sample Word	Invented Spelling	Suggested Mini Lesson Level/Lesson
happily	happly	3/21, 4/20, 4/26
hot	hit	1/18, 2/3, 3/1
hint	hit	2/11
hit	het	1/21, 2/2, 3/2
let's	lets	3/16, 3/28
letter	lettr	4/7, 4/25, 5/15, 5/26, 6/9
light	lit	2/15, 3/4, 4/4
make	mak	1/25, 3/3, 4/1
mine	min	1/28, 2/15, 3/4
nut	not	1/19, 2/8
pause	pawse	3/9, 6/3
pet	pat	1/20, 2/7, 3/2
please	pease	2/10, 5/13
pond	pod	2/5, 2/11
ponies	ponys	3/21, 4/20
pool	pole	2/17
pump	pup	2/11, 3/25
rain	ran	1/29, 2/13, 3/3, 4/1
rain	rane	2/13, 3/3
range	rang	3/20, 4/10, 4/14
seed	sed	1/27, 2/14
snap	sap	1/31, 2/26
spent	spat	2/5, 2/11, 3/25
sick	sik	2/4, 4/9
spoken	spokn	4/25, 5/26, 6/9
stair	stear	3/26, 4/31
stamp	stap	1/31, 2/11, 3/25
stepped	stept	2/32, 3/15, 4/35, 5/19
suddenly	sudenly	3/15, 6/4
table	tabl	3/11, 4/7, 4/25, 5/15, 5/26, 6/9
then	than	1/20, 2/7, 3/2
note	not	1/26, 2/16, 3/3
whale	wale	1/33, 2/19
winter	wintr	4/7, 4/25, 5/26, 6/9
	wintar	
went	wat	2/5, 2/11, 3/25

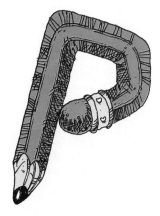

Answers for Crossword Puzzles

Pages T90-T95

Lesson 6, p.T90

ACROSS
3. flop
4. snack
6. rip
7. fat
8. gas
10. fix
12. stick
13. sand

DOWN
1. off
2. lock
4. spot
5. cross
7. fog
9. milk
11. kiss

Lesson 12, p.T91

ACROSS
3. mud
4. grin
5. us
6. sting
8. met
9. glass
10. tree
12. plus

DOWN
1. drive
2. rust
3. must
7. grade
8. mask
10. test
11. blast

Lesson 18, p.T92

ACROSS
1. plate
3. boat
5. wide
6. dream
10. soap
11. snow
13. wheel

DOWN
2. team
3. blow
4. read
7. sheep
8. moon
9. row
10. sight
12. deep

Lesson 24, p. T93

ACROSS
3. every
5. give
7. hard
9. does
11. shame
12. cart
13. park

DOWN
1. thing
2. were
4. your
6. where
8. dark
10. start
11. sharp
14. art

Lesson 30, p.T94

ACROSS
3. rode
4. bright
6. train
9. die
10. animals
12. meat
13. baby
14. sister
15. slip

DOWN
1. speech
2. deer
5. grandmother
7. frisky
8. sea
11. snakes

Lesson 36, p.T95

ACROSS
2. clown
4. batting
6. now
7. something
13. mopped
14. full

DOWN
1. town
2. cut
3. maybe
5. house
8. myself
9. ten
10. eight
11. good
12. foot

Answers for Review Tests

Pages T96-T101

Lesson 6, p. T96	Lesson 12, p. T97	Lesson 18, p. T98	Lesson 24, p. T99	Lesson 30, p. T100	Lesson 36, p. T101
1. b	1. c	1. a	1. b	1. b	1. c
2. b	2. a	2. a	2. c	2. c	2. a
3. c	3. a	3. c	3. b	3. b	3. a
4. a	4. c	4. b	4. a	4. c	4. c
5. b	5. a	5. c	5. c	5. a	5. b
6. a	6. b	6. c	6. c	6. b	6. a
7. c	7. c	7. a	7. b	7. a	7. a
8. c	8. b	8. c	8. b	8. b	8. b
9. a	9. c	9. b	9. b	9. a	9. b
10. a	10. a	10. a	10. c	10. c	10. a
11. c	11. b	11. c	11. a	11. c	11. c
12. c	12. a	12. b	12. c	12. b	12. b
13. c	13. a	13. a	13. a	13. b	13. c
14. c	14. c	14. b	14. b	14. a	14. c
15. b	15. b	15. c	15. a	15. a	15. c
16. a	16. c	16. b	16. a	16. a	16. b
17. a	17. b	17. a	17. b	17. c	17. c
18. c	18. a	18. b	18. c	18. c	18. a
19. b	19. b	19. a	19. a	19. a	19. b
20. a	20. c	20. b	20. c	20. c	20. a

SRA SPELLING *Lesson 6*

Name _____

Use Core Words from Lessons 1-5 to complete this puzzle.

ACROSS
3. to flap loosely
4. food between meals
6. tear
7. not thin
8. fuel for car
10. mend or repair
12. thin wood
13. use a bucket and shovel with this

DOWN
1. ___ and on
2. has its own key
4. a stain
5. to go from one side to another
7. mist
9. something you drink
11. touch with lips

SRA SPELLING *Lesson 12*

Name _____

Use Core Words from Lessons 7-11 to complete this puzzle.

ACROSS
- **3.** wet dirt
- **4.** smile
- **5.** you and me
- **6.** a bee does this
- **8.** rhymes with *pet*
- **9.** holds a drink
- **10.** it has a trunk
- **12.** two ____ two is four

DOWN
- **1.** ____ a car
- **2.** rhymes with *dust*
- **3.** have to
- **7.** you're in one in school
- **8.** worn on Halloween
- **10.** a spelling ____
- **11.** ____ off

Name _____

Use Core Words from Lessons 13-17 to complete this puzzle.

ACROSS
1. a dish
3. floats on water
5. broad
6. when you sleep
10. used with water
11. type of flake
13. spins around

DOWN
2. baseball group
3. ___ a bubble
4. ___ a book
7. old lamb
8. I come out at night.
9. moves boat across water
10. to see
12. way down

Name _____

Use Core Words from
Lessons 19-23 to complete
this puzzle.

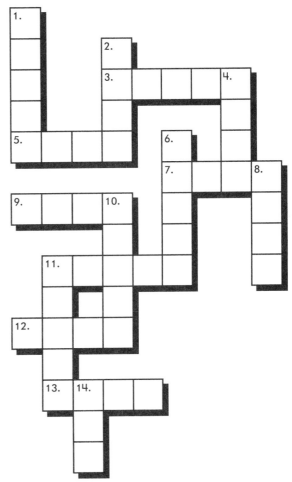

ACROSS

3. all
5. Please ____ it to me.
7. not soft but ____
9. I do; he ____.
11. a sorry feeling
12. a grocery ____
13. a place for fun

DOWN

1. rhymes with *ring*
2. We ____ not ready.
4. Is this ____ hat?
6. question word about place
8. opposite of *light*
10. This means to begin.
11. The knife has a ____ point.
14. crayons and paint are tools for this

Name _____

Use Core Words from
Lessons 25-29 to complete
this puzzle.

ACROSS
3. He ____ his bike.
4. The light is ____.
6. rhymes with *brain*
9. A plant without water will do this.
10. birds, fish, cows
12. food from animals
13. young child
14. not a brother, a _____
15. ____ and slide

DOWN
1. The president gave a _____.
2. A male _____ has antlers.
5. your mother's mother
7. bouncy and playful
8. ocean
11. reptiles without arms or legs

SRA SPELLING *Lesson 36*

Name _____

Use Core Words from Lessons 31-35 to complete this puzzle.

ACROSS

2. performs with a circus
4. swinging the bat
6. Right ___!
7. thing not known
13. He _____ the floor.
14. not empty

DOWN

1. small city
2. divide with a knife
3. perhaps
5. rhymes with *mouse*
8. my own self
9. after nine is ___
10. This number rhymes with *late.*
11. We had a ____ time.
12. it has toes

SRA SPELLING *Review Test Lesson 6*

Name _____

Each item below gives three possible spellings of a word. Choose the correct spelling. Mark your answer.

Answers

Sample.	a. tiger	b. tigur	c. tieger	●	(b)	(c)
1.	a. gis	b. gas	c. gase	1. (a)	(b)	(c)
2.	a. snak	b. snack	c. snac	2. (a)	(b)	(c)
3.	a. het	b. hayt	c. hat	3. (a)	(b)	(c)
4.	a. map	b. mep	c. mape	4. (a)	(b)	(c)
5.	a. los	b. lost	c. lohst	5. (a)	(b)	(c)
6.	a. milk	b. mylk	c. milke	6. (a)	(b)	(c)
7.	a. kyss	b. kus	c. kiss	7. (a)	(b)	(c)
8.	a. stacke	b. stak	c. stack	8. (a)	(b)	(c)
9.	a. spot	b. spet	c. spaht	9. (a)	(b)	(c)
10.	a. dog	b. dag	c. dawg	10. (a)	(b)	(c)
11.	a. laht	b. lat	c. lot	11. (a)	(b)	(c)
12.	a. laste	b. lat	c. last	12. (a)	(b)	(c)
13.	a. fas	b. fust	c. fast	13. (a)	(b)	(c)
14.	a. sik	b. syck	c. sick	14. (a)	(b)	(c)
15.	a. hes	b. his	c. hys	15. (a)	(b)	(c)
16.	a. mad	b. med	c. nad	16. (a)	(b)	(c)
17.	a. pond	b. pind	c. pand	17. (a)	(b)	(c)
18.	a. typ	b. tep	c. tip	18. (a)	(b)	(c)
19.	a. jub	b. job	c. jahb	19. (a)	(b)	(c)
20.	a. lock	b. loack	c. locke	20. (a)	(b)	(c)

SRA SPELLING *Review Test Lesson 12*

Name _____

Each item below gives three possible spellings of a word. Choose the correct spelling. Mark your answer.

Answers

Sample. a. tiger   b. tigur   c. tieger   ● (b) (c)

#	a.	b.	c.		Answers
1.	a. ruge	b. reg	c. rug	1.	(a) (b) (c)
2.	a. egg	b. ag	c. eeg	2.	(a) (b) (c)
3.	a. test	b. tast	c. tste	3.	(a) (b) (c)
4.	a. weng	b. wung	c. wing	4.	(a) (b) (c)
5.	a. mud	b. mid	c. med	5.	(a) (b) (c)
6.	a. yat	b. yet	c. yte	6.	(a) (b) (c)
7.	a. sone	b. seng	c. song	7.	(a) (b) (c)
8.	a. stuk	b. stuck	c. stcuk	8.	(a) (b) (c)
9.	a. durm	b. drem	c. drum	9.	(a) (b) (c)
10.	a. camp	b. canp	c. kamp	10.	(a) (b) (c)
11.	a. tre	b. tree	c. trae	11.	(a) (b) (c)
12.	a. truck	b. trock	c. truk	12.	(a) (b) (c)
13.	a. plus	b. plas	c. plos	13.	(a) (b) (c)
14.	a. blen	b. blnd	c. blend	14.	(a) (b) (c)
15.	a. gled	b. glad	c. gald	15.	(a) (b) (c)
16.	a. blst	b. blet	c. blast	16.	(a) (b) (c)
17.	a. dask	b. desk	c. dest	17.	(a) (b) (c)
18.	a. grin	b. girn	c. gren	18.	(a) (b) (c)
19.	a. luk	b. luck	c. luc	19.	(a) (b) (c)
20.	a. sind	b. synd	c. send	20.	(a) (b) (c)

Review Test Lesson 18

Name _____

Each item below gives three possible spellings of a word. Choose the correct spelling. Mark your answer.

Answers

Sample.	a. tiger	b. tigur	c. tieger	● b c

	a	b	c		a	b	c
1.	a. moon	b. mon	c. monn	1.	a	b	c
2.	a. plate	b. plat	c. plaet	2.	a	b	c
3.	a. bate	b. biat	c. bait	3.	a	b	c
4.	a. sey	b. say	c. saey	4.	a	b	c
5.	a. mael	b. mell	c. meal	5.	a	b	c
6.	a. treet	b. tret	c. treat	6.	a	b	c
7.	a. deep	b. deap	c. dep	7.	a	b	c
8.	a. zuu	b. zue	c. zoo	8.	a	b	c
9.	a. noes	b. nose	c. nos	9.	a	b	c
10.	a. dry	b. dri	c. dy	10.	a	b	c
11.	a. nite	b. niet	c. night	11.	a	b	c
12.	a. rite	b. right	c. riit	12.	a	b	c
13.	a. tune	b. tun	c. tuen	13.	a	b	c
14.	a. sope	b. soap	c. sopa	14.	a	b	c
15.	a. bloe	b. blo	c. blow	15.	a	b	c
16.	a. pien	b. pine	c. pyne	16.	a	b	c
17.	a. boat	b. bot	c. baot	17.	a	b	c
18.	a. sheap	b. sheep	c. seep	18.	a	b	c
19.	a. came	b. caem	c. kame	19.	a	b	c
20.	a. roon	b. room	c. rom	20.	a	b	c

Review Test Lesson 24

Name _____

Each item below gives three possible spellings of a word. Choose the correct spelling. Mark your answer.

Answers

					Answers		
Sample.	a. tiger	b. tigur	c. tieger		●	b	c
1.	a. wher	b. where	c. whare	1.	a	b	c
2.	a. verry	b. vere	c. very	2.	a	b	c
3.	a. fash	b. flash	c. flahs	3.	a	b	c
4.	a. shore	b. shoer	c. shor	4.	a	b	c
5.	a. gurl	b. gril	c. girl	5.	a	b	c
6.	a. buth	b. baht	c. bath	6.	a	b	c
7.	a. yur	b. your	c. yeer	7.	a	b	c
8.	a. thon	b. thin	c. tine	8.	a	b	c
9.	a. evry	b. every	c. aevry	9.	a	b	c
10.	a. darc	b. darck	c. dark	10.	a	b	c
11.	a. park	b. parq	c. parck	11.	a	b	c
12.	a. sherp	b. shrap	c. sharp	12.	a	b	c
13.	a. teach	b. teech	c. tech	13.	a	b	c
14.	a. frist	b. first	c. ferst	14.	a	b	c
15.	a. short	b. shote	c. shor	15.	a	b	c
16.	a. more	b. mure	c. moare	16.	a	b	c
17.	a. cert	b. cart	c. kart	17.	a	b	c
18.	a. geve	b. giv	c. give	18.	a	b	c
19.	a. tooth	b. toth	c. tuth	19.	a	b	c
20.	a. klash	b. clas	c. clash	20.	a	b	c

SRA SPELLING *Review Test Lesson 30*

Name _____

Each item below gives three possible spellings of a word. Choose the correct spelling. Mark your answer.

Answers

Sample. a. tiger   b. tigur   c. tieger   ● (b) (c)

#	a	b	c	Answer
1.	a. rowd	b. rode	c. roed	(a) (b) (c)
2.	a. brome	b. brum	c. broom	(a) (b) (c)
3.	a. forg	b. frog	c. frag	(a) (b) (c)
4.	a. trin	b. trian	c. train	(a) (b) (c)
5.	a. sled	b. slad	c. slead	(a) (b) (c)
6.	a. uncil	b. uncle	c. uncel	(a) (b) (c)
7.	a. spin	b. spen	c. spene	(a) (b) (c)
8.	a. spi	b. spy	c. spie	(a) (b) (c)
9.	a. see	b. se	c. sae	(a) (b) (c)
10.	a. bruther	b. brouther	c. brother	(a) (b) (c)
11.	a. ducs	b. duks	c. ducks	(a) (b) (c)
12.	a. whaels	b. whales	c. whals	(a) (b) (c)
13.	a. ents	b. ants	c. aynts	(a) (b) (c)
14.	a. dye	b. di	c. dey	(a) (b) (c)
15.	a. father	b. farher	c. farthar	(a) (b) (c)
16.	a. brag	b. braag	c. brage	(a) (b) (c)
17.	a. famly	b. faimly	c. family	(a) (b) (c)
18.	a. maet	b. mete	c. meat	(a) (b) (c)
19.	a. cows	b. caws	c. cau	(a) (b) (c)
20.	a. spase	b. spaec	c. space	(a) (b) (c)

SPELLING *Review Test Lesson 36*

Name _____

Each item below gives three possible spellings of a word. Choose the correct spelling. Mark your answer.

Answers

Sample. a. tiger   b. tigur   c. tieger   ● ⓑ ⓒ

#	a	b	c	Answers
1.	a. poush	b. puse	c. push	1. ⓐ ⓑ ⓒ
2.	a. four	b. fuor	c. foure	2. ⓐ ⓑ ⓒ
3.	a. book	b. buk	c. booc	3. ⓐ ⓑ ⓒ
4.	a. gud	b. gude	c. good	4. ⓐ ⓑ ⓒ
5.	a. bating	b. batting	c. battng	5. ⓐ ⓑ ⓒ
6.	a. eight	b. ight	c. eiht	6. ⓐ ⓑ ⓒ
7.	a. lunchroom	b. lunchrome	c. luncroom	7. ⓐ ⓑ ⓒ
8.	a. taaped	b. tapped	c. tapd	8. ⓐ ⓑ ⓒ
9.	a. ol	b. owl	c. owle	9. ⓐ ⓑ ⓒ
10.	a. down	b. dowe	c. doun	10. ⓐ ⓑ ⓒ
11.	a. towe	b. tou	c. two	11. ⓐ ⓑ ⓒ
12.	a. howse	b. house	c. howze	12. ⓐ ⓑ ⓒ
13.	a. mabe	b. maybee	c. maybe	13. ⓐ ⓑ ⓒ
14.	a. moped	b. mooped	c. mopped	14. ⓐ ⓑ ⓒ
15.	a. noteboke	b. noetbook	c. notebook	15. ⓐ ⓑ ⓒ
16.	a. somethng	b. something	c. somthing	16. ⓐ ⓑ ⓒ
17.	a. clonw	b. clon	c. clown	17. ⓐ ⓑ ⓒ
18.	a. full	b. ful	c. fule	18. ⓐ ⓑ ⓒ
19.	a. siks	b. six	c. sic	19. ⓐ ⓑ ⓒ
20.	a. cutting	b. cuting	c. kutting	20. ⓐ ⓑ ⓒ

1 Spelling the Short *a* Sound

CORE

1. lap
2. man
3. hat
4. map
5. has
6. pat
7. mad
8. gas
9. fat
10. bad

CHALLENGE

11. as
12. jam
13. dash
14. path
15. cash

WORDS FROM READING AND WRITING

16. _____
17. _____
18. _____
19. _____
20. _____

2 Spelling the Short *i* Sound

CORE

1. if
2. fix
3. pin
4. his
5. mix
6. rip
7. kiss
8. hid
9. tip
10. milk

CHALLENGE

11. dish
12. mitt
13. fish
14. rich
15. wish

WORDS FROM READING AND WRITING

16. _____
17. _____
18. _____
19. _____
20. _____

3 Spelling the /o/ and /ô/ Sounds

CORE

1. log
2. got
3. dog
4. job
5. lot
6. fog
7. flop
8. spot
9. jog
10. off

CHALLENGE

11. robin
12. soggy
13. slot
14. cross
15. cot

WORDS FROM READING AND WRITING

16. _____
17. _____
18. _____
19. _____
20. _____

4 Spelling the Final /k/ Sound

CORE

1. rock
2. kick
3. sack
4. dock
5. pack
6. sick
7. stack
8. lock
9. stick
10. snack

CHALLENGE

11. click
12. flock
13. shack
14. clock
15. backpack

WORDS FROM READING AND WRITING

16. _____
17. _____
18. _____
19. _____
20. _____

5 Spelling the /nd/ and /st/ Sounds

CORE

1. sand
2. pond
3. lost
4. just
5. and
6. last
7. list
8. band
9. fast
10. hand

CHALLENGE

11. cast
12. stand
13. past
14. wind
15. land

WORDS FROM READING AND WRITING

16. _____

17. _____

18. _____

19. _____

20. _____

7 Spelling the Short e Sound

CORE

1. egg
2. fed
3. met
4. them
5. rest
6. bend
7. yet
8. test
9. went
10. send

CHALLENGE

11. pen
12. mess
13. stem
14. mend
15. west

WORDS FROM READING AND WRITING

16. _____

17. _____

18. _____

19. _____

20. _____

8 Spelling the Short *u* Sound

CORE

1. us
2. mud
3. rub
4. tug
5. luck
6. must
7. rug
8. shut
9. rust
10. stuck

CHALLENGE

11. dust
12. hush
13. lunch
14. rush
15. bunch

WORDS FROM READING AND WRITING

16. _____

17. _____

18. _____

19. _____

20. _____

9 Spelling Words with *dr, tr,* and *gr*

CORE

1. drip
2. grin
3. tree
4. drum
5. grade
6. trip
7. drive
8. grand
9. truck
10. drove

CHALLENGE

11. dress
12. trim
13. grass
14. try
15. grow

WORDS FROM READING AND WRITING

16. _____

17. _____

18. _____

19. _____

20. _____

10 Spelling Words with *gl*, *bl*, and *pl*

CORE

1. blast
2. glad
3. plan
4. blend
5. plus
6. glass
7. plum
8. blink
9. plot
10. block

CHALLENGE

11. glue
12. blank
13. planet
14. gloves
15. blanket

WORDS FROM READING AND WRITING

16. _____

17. _____

18. _____

19. _____

20. _____

11 Spelling Words That End with *sk*, *mp*, and *ng*

CORE

1. mask
2. camp
3. long
4. ask
5. sting
6. dump
7. wing
8. desk
9. song
10. jump

CHALLENGE

11. blimp
12. task
13. stamp
14. bring
15. grump

WORDS FROM READING AND WRITING

16. _____

17. _____

18. _____

19. _____

20. _____

13 Spelling the Long *a* Sound

CORE

1. rake
2. bait
3. say
4. cane
5. pail
6. hay
7. plate
8. raise
9. came
10. grape

CHALLENGE

11. trail
12. blaze
13. pain
14. tray
15. stain

WORDS FROM READING AND WRITING

16. _____
17. _____
18. _____
19. _____
20. _____

14 Spelling the Long *e* Sound

CORE

1. read
2. each
3. seen
4. wheel
5. team
6. deep
7. meal
8. treat
9. dream
10. sheep

CHALLENGE

11. mean
12. cream
13. sneeze
14. leave
15. sleep

WORDS FROM READING AND WRITING

16. _____
17. _____
18. _____
19. _____
20. _____

15 Spelling the Long *i* Sound

CORE

1. pine
2. night
3. cry
4. fight
5. wide
6. fly
7. light
8. sight
9. dry
10. right

CHALLENGE

11. sly
12. might
13. stripe
14. shy
15. tight

WORDS FROM READING AND WRITING

16. _____

17. _____

18. _____

19. _____

20. _____

16 Spelling the Long *o* Sound

CORE

1. coat
2. blow
3. nose
4. boat
5. row
6. those
7. goat
8. soap
9. snow
10. toad

CHALLENGE

11. slow
12. coach
13. float
14. globe
15. toast

WORDS FROM READING AND WRITING

16. _____

17. _____

18. _____

19. _____

20. _____

17 Spelling the /ü/ Sound

CORE

1. tube
2. zoo
3. boot
4. food
5. tune
6. pool
7. soon
8. rude
9. moon
10. room

CHALLENGE

11. moose
12. cute
13. balloon
14. shoot
15. goose

WORDS FROM READING AND WRITING

16. _____
17. _____
18. _____
19. _____
20. _____

19 Spelling Words with *wh* and *sh*

CORE

1. what
2. clash
3. shame
4. why
5. shine
6. flash
7. shock
8. where
9. shore
10. while

CHALLENGE

11. whisper
12. shall
13. share
14. whiskers
15. shadow

WORDS FROM READING AND WRITING

16. _____
17. _____
18. _____
19. _____
20. _____

20 Spelling Words with *ch* and *th*

CORE

1. much
2. thing
3. such
4. choke
5. tooth
6. thank
7. bath
8. thin
9. teach
10. with

CHALLENGE

11. child
12. thick
13. reach
14. chore
15. think

WORDS FROM READING AND WRITING

16. _____
17. _____
18. _____
19. _____
20. _____

21 Spelling the Vowel + *r* Sound

CORE

1. farm
2. cart
3. dark
4. yard
5. art
6. barn
7. park
8. start
9. hard
10. sharp

CHALLENGE

11. arm
12. march
13. alarm
14. smart
15. harm

WORDS FROM READING AND WRITING

16. _____
17. _____
18. _____
19. _____
20. _____

22 Spelling More Vowel + *r* Sounds

CORE

1. girl
2. more
3. bird
4. horse
5. dirt
6. horn
7. short
8. first
9. for
10. shirt

CHALLENGE

11. store
12. third
13. morning
14. dinosaur
15. whirl

WORDS FROM READING AND WRITING

16. _____
17. _____
18. _____
19. _____
20. _____

23 Easily Misspelled Words

CORE

1. does
2. gone
3. who
4. any
5. your
6. give
7. very
8. were
9. live
10. every

CHALLENGE

11. many
12. away
13. goes
14. kind
15. both

WORDS FROM READING AND WRITING

16. _____
17. _____
18. _____
19. _____
20. _____

25 Spelling Words with *br*, *fr*, and *tr*

CORE

1. train
2. brag
3. free
4. trade
5. frog
6. brick
7. frisky
8. bright
9. trick
10. broom

CHALLENGE

11. front
12. bread
13. tramp
14. friend
15. treat

WORDS FROM READING AND WRITING

16. _____

17. _____

18. _____

19. _____

20. _____

26 Spelling Words with *sl* and *sp*

CORE

1. slam
2. spin
3. speed
4. slip
5. space
6. slide
7. slick
8. speech
9. spy
10. sled

CHALLENGE

11. spoon
12. slant
13. speak
14. spark
15. spoke

WORDS FROM READING AND WRITING

16. _____

17. _____

18. _____

19. _____

20. _____

27 Spelling Words Ending with -s

CORE

1. ducks
2. cows
3. whales
4. seals
5. rabbits
6. ants
7. chickens
8. zebras
9. snakes
10. animals

CHALLENGE

11. lions
12. bears
13. tigers
14. chipmunks
15. kangaroos

WORDS FROM READING AND WRITING

16. _____

17. _____

18. _____

19. _____

20. _____

28 Spelling Words That Sound Alike

CORE

1. see
2. sea
3. dear
4. deer
5. meet
6. meat
7. road
8. rode
9. dye
10. die

CHALLENGE

11. seam
12. seem
13. eye
14. too
15. to

WORDS FROM READING AND WRITING

16. _____

17. _____

18. _____

19. _____

20. _____

29 Spelling Family Names

CORE

1. family
2. mother
3. sister
4. grandmother
5. aunt
6. baby
7. grandfather
8. uncle
9. father
10. brother

CHALLENGE

11. parent
12. children
13. together
14. person
15. twins

WORDS FROM READING AND WRITING

16. _____
17. _____
18. _____
19. _____
20. _____

31 Spelling the /u/ Sound

CORE

1. put
2. hook
3. full
4. took
5. push
6. foot
7. book
8. pull
9. look
10. good

CHALLENGE

11. crook
12. stood
13. shook
14. wool
15. cookbook

WORDS FROM READING AND WRITING

16. _____
17. _____
18. _____
19. _____
20. _____

32 Spelling Words Ending in *-ed* and *-ing*

CORE

1. mop
2. mopped
3. hit
4. hitting
5. bat
6. batting
7. tap
8. tapped
9. cut
10. cutting

CHALLENGE

11. running
12. skipping
13. digging
14. hopping
15. begged

WORDS FROM READING AND WRITING

16. _____
17. _____
18. _____
19. _____
20. _____

33 Spelling the /ou/ Sound

CORE

1. out
2. now
3. clown
4. our
5. down
6. sound
7. owl
8. house
9. town
10. loud

CHALLENGE

11. found
12. howl
13. south
14. crown
15. around

WORDS FROM READING AND WRITING

16. _____
17. _____
18. _____
19. _____
20. _____

34 Spelling Compound Words

CORE

1. maybe
2. bedroom
3. lunchroom
4. into
5. something
6. nobody
7. doghouse
8. myself
9. inside
10. notebook

CHALLENGE

11. sailboat
12. downtown
13. weekend
14. everywhere
15. sandbox

WORDS FROM READING AND WRITING

16. _____
17. _____
18. _____
19. _____
20. _____

35 Spelling Number Words

CORE

1. one
2. two
3. three
4. four
5. five
6. six
7. seven
8. eight
9. nine
10. ten

CHALLENGE

11. count
12. add
13. numbers
14. minus
15. second

WORDS FROM READING AND WRITING

16. _____
17. _____
18. _____
19. _____
20. _____

Test-Study-Test

Lesson _____

	Pretest	Self Check and Correct	Retest
1.	_____	_____	_____
2.	_____	_____	_____
3.	_____	_____	_____
4.	_____	_____	_____
5.	_____	_____	_____
6.	_____	_____	_____
7.	_____	_____	_____
8.	_____	_____	_____
9.	_____	_____	_____
10.	_____	_____	_____
11.	_____	_____	_____
12.	_____	_____	_____
13.	_____	_____	_____
14.	_____	_____	_____
15.	_____	_____	_____

SPELLING Student Progress Chart

Name _____

Percent Correct

Percent
Correct

100
95
90
85
80
75
70
65
60
55
50
45
40
35
30
25
20
15
10
5
0

Lesson 1 2 3 4 5 6 7 8 9 10 11 12 13 14 15 16 17 18 19 20 21 22 23 24 25 26 27 28 29 30 31 32 33 34 35 36

Number Correct

	Pretest	Retest
Lesson 1	_____	_____
Lesson 2	_____	_____
Lesson 3	_____	_____
Lesson 4	_____	_____
Lesson 5	_____	_____
Lesson 6	_____	_____
Lesson 7	_____	_____
Lesson 8	_____	_____
Lesson 9	_____	_____
Lesson 10	_____	_____
Lesson 11	_____	_____
Lesson 12	_____	_____
Lesson 13	_____	_____
Lesson 14	_____	_____
Lesson 15	_____	_____
Lesson 16	_____	_____
Lesson 17	_____	_____
Lesson 18	_____	_____
Lesson 19	_____	_____
Lesson 20	_____	_____
Lesson 21	_____	_____
Lesson 22	_____	_____
Lesson 23	_____	_____
Lesson 24	_____	_____
Lesson 25	_____	_____
Lesson 26	_____	_____
Lesson 27	_____	_____
Lesson 28	_____	_____
Lesson 29	_____	_____
Lesson 30	_____	_____
Lesson 31	_____	_____
Lesson 32	_____	_____
Lesson 33	_____	_____
Lesson 34	_____	_____
Lesson 35	_____	_____
Lesson 36	_____	_____